EUROPE

6.26
B+T
3-31-87

WORLD ALMANAC'S

LEGAL GUIDE FOR

AMERICAN

TRAVELERS

346.73 N858w   c.1
Novik, Jack.   110101   000
World almanac's legal guide fo

3 9311 00073986 8
GRACE COLL/SEM-MORGAN LIBRARY

EUROPE

WORLD ALMANAC'S
LEGAL GUIDE FOR
AMERICAN
TRAVELERS

JACK D. NOVIK

GRACE COLLEGE LIBRARY
Winona Lake, Indiana
46590

WORLD ALMANAC PUBLICATIONS
NEW YORK, NEW YORK

Cover and text design by Elyse Strongin
Copyright © 1986 by Jack D. Novik

All rights reserved. No part of this book may be reproduced in any
means without written permission of the publisher.

First published in 1986

Distributed in the United States by Ballantine Books, a division of
Random House, Inc. and in Canada by Random House of Canada,
Ltd.

Library of Congress Catalog Card Number: 85-052238
Newpaper Enterprise Association ISBN: 0-88687-256-1
Ballantine Books ISBN: 0-345-33307-1

Printed in the United States of America
World Almanac Publications
Newspaper Enterprise Association
A division of United Media Enterprises
A Scripps Howard Company
200 Park Avenue
New York, NY 10166
10 9 8 7 6 5 4 3 2 1

TO: M.A.

TABLE OF CONTENTS

IV. RETURNING TO THE UNITED STATES

V. APPENDICES

PREFACE

When I began this project I thought a legal guide for travelers would be useful to Americans only after trouble had struck. Why anticipate legal problems when there are so many pleasant things to think about before setting off on a trip to Western Europe?

As it happens, I was both right and wrong: there are many agreeable aspects of travel, but they are best enjoyed by the well-prepared traveler. It is significant that the word travel is derived from travail (meaning agony and hard work), which comes from the Latin word tripalium: an instrument of torture. Every seasoned traveler knows that even a modicum of planning and foresight can provide just that measure of protection necessary to prevent your travel experience from degenerating into torture and making you its victim.

In preparing this book, I traveled throughout Western Europe speaking mostly to the people who take care of Americans in trouble—U.S. consulate officials, lawyers, local police, and travel advisers. The information included here is the best available to me at the time of writing. However, you must keep in mind that laws, rules, regulations, and law-enforcement priorities change over time. This is particularly so with respect to criminal laws, such as drug offenses, which are being revised dramatically throughout Western Europe.

Therefore, this book must be used as a resource to alert you to possible limits on your conduct, rather than as the final word on what those limits are. For example, if a country has a currency export restriction and you are traveling with considerably less than the amount listed in the book, it is safe to assume you will still be within appropriate limits even a few years from now—these restrictions tend not to vary drastically in Western Europe in the short term. But if you were traveling with only a few dollars less than the restriction indicated, it would be best to make an inquiry of the appropriate official to determine if there has been any change in the rule, because even a small change might put you over the limit.

For the most part, safe travel is a matter of common sense. There is no need—particularly in Western Europe— to be obsessed with every last detailed technicality of the law. It does make sense, however, to appreciate that you are going to be in places with laws and customs different from those that govern your life at home. And you are not relieved from obeying those laws and respecting those customs just because you are an American.

Be careful, have fun, and enjoy your trip.

Jack Novik
Summer 1985

ACKNOWLEDGEMENTS

I could not have written this book without the help of a great many strangers who assisted me in researching the details, as well as a few good friends whose support enabled me to do the research that was necessary. I wish to thank them all.

Much of the raw data for this book came from U.S. government sources, in particular from employees of the State Department's Bureau of Consular Affairs. Almost without exception, they were enormously helpful, informative, and indulgent of my repeated inquiries. I particularly want to express my appreciation to the consulate officials—both American Foreign Service officers and foreign national employees—I interviewed throughout Western Europe. They have a very hard job—dealing with people in all manner of crisis situations is both professionally and emotionally demanding—and they do it with skill and sensitivity. Their experience, resourcefulness, and insight were invaluable to me in writing this book, as they should be to you if you are ever in need of help abroad.

I also relied heavily on local lawyers, government officials, and travel professionals in each of the countries I visited. For the most part, I did not know any of these people in advance. Typically, I obtained their names from the American consulate, called them without introduction, and asked for help. I was never refused. In appreciation I had intended to list each of them by name. Ironically, however, though I traveled all over Western Europe without a single unpleasant incident, upon my return, my home was burglarized, and among the things lost were my records of those people who had been so helpful to me in Europe. I therefore take this opportunity to thank them for their unselfish assistance, and hope they will forgive me for not being able to acknowledge them individually for their gracious, though brief, friendship.

And of course I am indebted to my friends (including a few relatives) in this country who helped me with this project:

Connie Mann, in its conception; my uncle Morris Novik and Ernest Lee with its logistics; my daughter Jenifer Novik by enduring my absence gracefully, if not happily; my colleagues at the American Civil Liberties Union with their enthusiasm; and my parents by giving their confidence and support. My brother Neil Novik and my good friend Jonathan Siegfried were especially important to me for their reservoirs of strength, intelligence, and good cheer.

Lastly, this book would never have been started, and could not have been finished, but for the ever affectionate prodding of Mary Ann Frank and George Sheanshang. George is a dear friend, a talented writer, and a shrewd lawyer and adviser—I ask more of him than I should and he willingly gives more than that. Mary Ann, too, has been friend, kibitzer and confidante throughout. Her involvement in my life has heightened the pleasures of this undertaking for me, and she has shouldered more of its load than the dedication of this book to her can convey.

EUROPE

WORLD ALMANAC'S
LEGAL GUIDE FOR
AMERICAN
TRAVELERS

I

U.S. CONSULAR SERVICES

When an American is in trouble overseas, the U.S. consulate usually receives the first call for help. Whether the difficulty is as routine (though not unimportant) as a stolen passport, as traumatic as the death of a traveling companion, or as serious as being arrested on criminal charges, the American typically looks to the consulate for more than just bureaucratic processing.

The consulate is a source of comfort because it speaks your language. It is a source of strength because it is on your side. It is a reassuring symbol of the power of your government ready to come to your defense. In short, the consulate is the closest available substitute for the safety and familiarity of home.

It is all too easy to believe that the consulate can solve all of your problems. Usually, it cannot.

The degree to which the consulate's services satisfy the American looking to the consulate for help depends not only on what the consulate is actually empowered to do for the American in trouble but also on what the traveler expects the consulate to do. It also depends on the skill and sensitivity of the consular officials handling the matter. Before describing the consular services available to Americans in trouble, a few words are in order about some of the practical limitations Americans may encounter in dealing with our consulates.

---

1. GETTING IN TROUBLE ABROAD

Americans who have found themselves in trouble abroad— any kind of trouble, from the relatively minor to the most serious—often complain that they did not receive the help they had expected from the American consulate.

In part, that disappointment may result from misinformed notions of the consulate's powers. The consulate frequently just cannot do what the American wants or needs. But all too often the American is dissatisfied because consulate officials do not do what they can and should do to help, because they feel too busy or because they have become bureaucrats—in the worst sense—and have lost touch with the people they are supposed to help.

In either case, the knowledgeable traveler will avoid a great deal of aggravation (and perhaps might be especially aware to avoid trouble in the first place) if mindful of the following considerations bearing on the consulate's ability to help.

1. Americans traveling in a foreign country are subject to the laws and legal procedures of that country. (The applicability of foreign law is treated at length in Section II: 7, 8.) The Constitutional rights and legal privileges we, as Americans, enjoy in this country do not protect us at all when we are in a foreign country, except if that country chooses to provide similar rights and privileges for its own nationals.

   Our Bill of Rights does not apply abroad. Our legal system, which is significantly different from most foreign systems, does not apply abroad. Our standards of bureaucratic service and governmental accountability—the ways in which we are accustomed to being treated—are not relevant to how we will be treated abroad.

   International law prohibits a country from treating Americans worse than its own nationals. But if a country chooses to treat its own citizens poorly by our standards, Americans are not entitled to be treated any better. And there is no formal action available to the consulate to obtain quicker, better, or more favorable treatment for the American in trouble. (Occasionally an "inquiry" from the consulate, or some "informal" assistance, can go a long way toward helping the American in trouble; however, whether the consular official will go that extra step to help is as much a function of personality and attitude as it is of legal power.)

2. The American in trouble quite naturally becomes preoccupied with the problem at hand and frequently comes to the consulate with expectations that far exceed the consulate's capabilities. To understand what this means, think about how you would deal with adversity if it happened to you in your hometown, in the United States.

   Whether your driver's license is stolen, or your spouse suffers a sudden incapacitating illness, or you are arrested on a criminal charge, you will likely call on several different resource networks for help. Family and friends can provide support, counsel, and protection. You will probably have at least one shoulder to cry on and a sympathetic ear to listen to your fear, anger, and frustration. In addition, federal, state, and local agencies are available for information and assistance services. Furthermore, you will have ways of finding reliable doctors, lawyers, and other professionals whom you can consult about your most pressing concerns. And, when the need warrants, religious and other advisers are at hand for guidance and comfort.

In a foreign country, however, you are alone. And while most people would say they understand that the consulate cannot play the role of lawyer, doctor, or family, nonetheless when trouble strikes, many people expect just such attention from the consulate staff. In many respects, this expectation is unreasonable, and the American who does not appreciate the consulate's limitations will almost certainly feel gravely disappointed.

3. When you are in trouble abroad, you will have to accept the fact that no one will think your difficulty is as important as you think it is. Even serious problems—such as illness, destitution, or arrest—are just routine incidents for the consulate staff, the local police, the hotel management, the hospital administrators, etc. To those people you are just the latest in a constant flow of tourists who suffer the same problems every week, every season, every year.

Of course, this is not to say that the people you turn to for help will be callous or indifferent, and you are certainly entitled to be treated courteously and efficiently regardless of how many other people have come before you. But you will rarely be serviced with the sense of urgency you feel the situation warrants.

4. Although consular officials around Western Europe seem consistently well versed in the rules and regulations governing consular matters—presumably because they all receive essentially the same training—they are not all equally well suited to the job. As a result, they are often the subject of a great deal of angry criticism by the very Americans they were supposed to have helped.

Consular officials, by definition, deal with Americans in trouble—people who are upset, scared, angry, injured, or functionally incapacitated by personal tragedy. Although we, as consulate clients, have to remember the limitations of consular services, an effective consular official must also be sensitive to the American's frayed condition and be able to appear concerned and interested even after hearing the same story from dozens of people year after year.

One of the best consular officials I met said, "Consular work is all about helping people. And anyone who does not enjoy helping people should not be in this business." It is an attitude about the work—a sensitivity to and an affinity for people—that distinguishes the truly capable and effective consular official.

As a rule, you will not be able to choose the person who handles your case if you are in need of consulate assistance. However, be aware that in addition to the U.S. Foreign Service officials, consulates are often staffed by local national employees who are generally first rate. They are not only knowledgeable about local practicalities but are also eager to be of help.

I have encountered Americans waiting at a consulate for help who thought that because a local employee was handling their case they were being given second-class treatment. They demanded to see an American official instead. In my experience, that is a mistake; frequently the best service you can get is from the foreign national employees.

5. Consular services are often limited by staff workloads and budgetary constraints. Although there has been an increase in the size of consular staffing, the State Department acknowledges that "the increased personnel has not kept pace with the rapid increase in workload." As a result, the consulate "cannot always provide the level of assistance desired by a distressed citizen or worried family." The problem may be particularly severe in the major tourist areas during the tourist season, just when the need is greatest, because the consulate officials are then most hard pressed to handle all of the requests made on their time and services.

6. The Privacy Act—a U.S. law designed, in part, to protect individual privacy rights—imposes certain important constraints on consular services. The general rule of the law is that information in the government's files about an individual may not be released to anyone—parents, close friends, even doctors—without that individual's express written consent. Thus, when an American is arrested in a foreign country and is visited by a consular official, one of the first questions asked is whether the American consents to the consulate's releasing information to family, friends, Congress, or the press. If the person does not grant permission and does not sign a Privacy Act waiver (see Appendix B), then no information will be released, even though this may cause considerable suffering for the worried family and friends who may have no other sources of information.

Similarly, if someone in your family, or a friend, is in trouble abroad, you cannot just call up the consulate to find out if that person is OK. Unless the American in trouble has expressly waived the Privacy Act, the consulate will tell you very little. Of course it may make sense to tell you, and of course you just want to help, but the consulate is powerless, and, though frustrating for you, it is counterproductive to be angry at the consulate for abiding by a good law that generally well serves the public interest.

2. HOW THE CONSULATE CAN HELP

Consular services are typically divided into three sections: visas, passports, and citizen services.

■ VISA SECTION

The Visa Section deals with foreigners seeking entry to the United States, and is thus rarely involved with the problems of Americans abroad. (Keep in mind, however, that one of the grievances Europeans harbor against Americans is that you, as an American, can generally travel freely through Western Europe for months without any visa at all, while Europeans cannot visit the United States even for a short vacation without first obtaining a visa. If you ever have occasion to visit an American consulate, the majority of people there will be foreign nationals applying for visas, and you will usually find them patiently annoyed by the time, hassle, and perceived unfairness of the American visa requirements.)

■ PASSPORT SECTION

The Passport Section is responsible for issuing new passports to Americans abroad, typically because their passports have been lost. (I use the word "lost" to mean stolen as well as misplaced passports.) Not only is the passport often lost along with other important papers (credit cards, traveler's checks, and money), but the process of replacing a passport can be an annoying and time-consuming distraction from the trip you had planned.

Although the United States requires that certain procedures be followed before a new passport can be issued—and sometimes these can be a hassle—most of the people I talked to felt that replacement passports were processed expeditiously and that red tape was kept to a minimum.

The first requirement for obtaining a replacement passport is that the loss of the original passport be reported to the local police. In most of the principal metropolitan areas of Western Europe, filing a police report does not present many difficulties. The police are accustomed to American travelers and frequently have English-speaking officers on duty to assist them. However, the police may be somewhat more difficult to deal with when you are traveling in places off the beaten track.

In any event, your copy of a police document, reflecting the report of a stolen passport, must be presented to the consulate to begin processing your request for a replacement.

The issuance of a passport overseas is subject to the same

requirements as passports issued in the United States. (In summary, those requirements include proving your U.S. citizenship, proving your identity, completing a passport application, and presenting two passport photographs.) However, there are some practical differences worth noting:

1. The State Department, concerned about the misuse of stolen passports, warns: "To protect the integrity of the U.S. passport and the security of the person bearing it, the Office of Passport Services has found it necessary to take special precautions in processing lost passport cases. These precautions, which include verification of the circumstances of loss as well as a review in the Department, may involve some delay before a new passport is issued."

2. One standard requirement—for your original as well as for any replacement passport—is proving citizenship and identity. Surprising as it seems, this can be more difficult than you might at first imagine, particularly if your wallet and other identification have been lost along with your passport.

   Identity may be established by appropriate documentation that includes a signature and a photograph or physical description—such as a driver's license or an identification card from work or school. (Note that the State Department specifically refuses to accept social security cards, credit cards, or cards reflecting membership in social organizations or clubs.) In addition, if you are traveling with someone carrying a U.S. passport, your spouse, for example, that person may attest to your identity.

   As a practical matter, the Foreign Service official handling the passport application has a great amount of discretion and, unless the circumstances are suspicious, will likely go out of the way to confirm citizenship and identity. However, this potential problem suggests the advisability of separating your important documents—so that in case of loss they will not all be gone at once—and leaving some pieces of identification, such as your voter registration card or driver's license, at your hotel.

   Once identity is established, the State Department is contacted to check the original passport number, date and place of issue. Therefore, it is a good idea to record that information apart from the passport itself, and to keep it with your credit card and traveler's check numbers. You might consider leaving all these numbers, including your passport number and information, with a friend or relative in the States whom you can call if necessary.

3. Another difficulty frequently encountered in obtaining a replacement passport is the need for passport photographs. Of course, each consulate can direct you to a local shop or

photograph machine where the photographs may be purchased (such machines are only very rarely available in the consulate itself). But if the shop is closed, or the machine is out of order, it can be quite a bother running around an unfamiliar city looking for a place to obtain two 2" x 2" passport photographs. Since most Americans have photos made before they leave the States (e.g., for passports, international driver's license), it would be wise to have a few extras made and to tuck them away in the luggage, apart from the passport itself, just for insurance.

■ CITIZEN SERVICES SECTION

Officials of the consular service boast that U.S. consulates provide greater assistance and protection to Americans abroad than any other country provides for its nationals. And that claim seems to be true. Still, Americans who find themselves in need of assistance are often dismayed at how limited consular services are. The difference between citizen expectation and consular performance usually comes down to this: the consulates generally cannot solve your problem for you; rather, the consulates are equipped to help you help yourself.

That theme of consular services—helping you to help yourself—repeats itself in virtually every circumstance:

- When you are arrested, the consulate cannot "get you off," or even legally represent you, but it can help you find an attorney, help you contact family and friends, and help you survive under reasonably humane conditions;

- When you are out of money, the consulate generally cannot cash your check or loan you money, but it can facilitate your contact with family and friends who can help;

- When you are sick, the consulate cannot provide medical evacuation home, but it can provide you or your family with substantial assistance in obtaining medical care abroad and making any necessary arrangements for evacuation.

Thus, each consulate knows the sources of local assistance —doctors, lawyers, and others—but cannot provide that assistance itself. The consulate can familiarize you with, and help you deal with, the local red tape, but it cannot eliminate it for you. In short, the consulate can facilitate the resolution of your difficulty, but it cannot resolve it for you.

Legal Problems. Each consulate maintains a list of local English-speaking lawyers, but the consulate usually emphasizes that it cannot vouch for the quality of the lawyers listed and that inclusion on the list does not constitute a recommendation by the consulate.

7

In fact, there do not seem to be any consistently applied practices governing the compilation of the lawyers' list. At some stations, virtually anyone who wants to be on the list can be; the list is updated infrequently and there is practically no quality control. Other stations, however, are more diligent in the maintenance of the list, updating it with some regularity, inquiring about quality, and removing lawyers who repeatedly provide inadequate services. Unfortunately, there is usually no way of learning anything about the characteristics of the list from the document itself. Rather, you will have to inquire of the consulate staff about how the list is compiled, whether it is current, and if quality control is maintained.

Although the consulate cannot make any formal recommendations, many of the more experienced consular officials will direct you to one or more of the lawyers on the list having especially good reputations. Frequently, obtaining the information depends on how you ask the question. Remember, the official you are talking to is, first, a bureaucrat who does not want to take any responsiblity, or to be blamed in any way, if things go wrong.

So the question, "Which lawyer do you recommend?" is likely to trigger the standard State Department response about not vouching for the quality of any lawyer.

However, questions like, "Is there one lawyer who seems especially experienced in this problem?" or, "Have you heard complaints about any of the lawyers on the list?" or, "Who would you go to if you had this problem?" all ask for factual information—reports of experience, past performance, or the official's own preference—rather than recommendations to you, so they may be safer for the official to answer. It is a small semantic difference, but it may be enough to elicit some helpful information.

In addition to the lawyers' list, many consulates prepare other useful handouts relating to legal matters. For example, some have a summary of the local criminal justice system (usually prepared by a local lawyer) for people who have been arrested. These handouts are not uniformly prepared in every consulate, and are not of uniform quality among the consulates that do prepare them. However, if you have a legal problem, it is always a good idea to check with the consulate to see if it has any written information or can otherwise provide you with any helpful leads.

Arrests. A person arrested in a foreign country is in serious trouble. Of course, being arrested anywhere is a grave problem, but when arrested abroad the American will be subject to local criminal justice procedures, which are likely to be largely unfamiliar. (See the discussion of these procedures in Section II: 7, 8, and the country-by-country listings in Section III.) And despite a popular myth, an American will not receive favored treatment just for being an American.

In other words, the fact that you are traveling on a U.S. passport will not get you off. Similarly, the consulate will not be able to get you out of jail simply by invoking the power of the United States.

As explained by the State Department, "the consular officer's role in arrest cases is one of observation and support." To the person in trouble, however, it often seems that the consulate is painfully passive, doing more observing than supporting. As so frequently is the case, much depends on the skill, sensitivity, and energy of the particular consular official.

Thus, while it is true that the consulate cannot free you from your predicament, a capable consular official can provide an enormous amount of assistance, both formally—within the constraints of official action—and informally—by "knowing the ropes."

Consular treaties require that when an American is arrested the consulate must be informed immediately. The countries of Western Europe usually adhere to this protocol without much difficulty, particularly with regard to arrests in the major cities, where the police authorities are accustomed to handling tourists. Occasionally, when an American is arrested in the provinces, where the police are less familiar with the requirements of consular treaties, it may take a few days before American authorities are notified.

Upon notification of an arrest, a consular official should visit the American at the earliest possible time. Usually, that first visit occurs within 48 hours of the arrest, although if the American is detained in a city distant from the consular city, the visit may take somewhat longer to arrange. In addition, local procedures may not permit consular or other visits until after an initial period of investigation.

During the first visit, the consular official will, typically:

- provide the arrested American with the list of lawyers;

- provide whatever written information the consulate has available about the criminal justice system;

- explain, generally from the consular official's experience, how the case is likely to proceed (although State Department officials emphasize that they do not, and cannot, give any legal advice);

- check on conditions of confinement and the health and welfare of the prisoner. Keep in mind that although conditions in local prisons may be deplorable, the consulate will not be able to arrange better accommodations so long as the American is receiving treatment comparable to what nationals of that country would receive;

9

- request instructions from the prisoner about whether the consulate may provide information to family, friends, Congress, or the press. Instructions permitting the release of information must be in the form of a written Privacy Act waiver, discussed above. (A sample Privacy Act Waiver Form is reproduced in Appendix B.)

Once an American is confined on a long-term basis, the consulate's role becomes that of overseer and liaison. During the course of imprisonment, a consulate official will regularly visit the prisoner. These visits typically occur about once a month, but may be more often if circumstances warrant, or less often if staff workload is heavy. One important purpose of these regular visits is to ensure that the American's health and welfare are not endangered. Certainly, if the prison conditions are so inadequate as to fall below civilized standards, the consulate can complain on behalf of the American prisoner and insist that conditions be improved. Moreover, although conditions in Western Europe are rarely bad enough to warrant a formal protest, an informal request by an American official may be of some help in alleviating the worst of the American's problems.

Another important consular function in these cases is to act as a channel of communication between the prisoner and family or friends (but only if the prisoner permits).

Generally, the feeding and medical care of prisoners are the responsibility of the prison authorities. In most prisons throughout Western Europe, these needs are adequately satisfied. However, if necessary, the consulate may be able to provide dietary supplements (''Care packages'' of food) and medical care to the prisoner. And in extreme cases, when outside food or medical care are essential but neither the prisoner nor concerned family have the necessary resources, a loan may be available for those purposes through the Emergency Medical and Dietary Assistance Program.

Lastly, the consulate may try to minimize the emotional toll of being imprisoned in a foreign jail by arranging for reading materials; attempting to facilitate family visits; providing personal amenities as stationery, postage stamps, and toiletries; and seeking the assistance of the local American community.

Civil Disputes. While traveling abroad, Americans can become involved in a variety of civil disputes (that is, disputes between an American and other individuals regarding property or personal injury claims). These disputes can range from substantial to very modest. For example, at one extreme, the personal and property damage claims resulting from a car accident may involve a good deal of money. Similarly, a merchant's failure to ship a valuable antique may cause a significant loss. On the other hand, a hotel bill dispute, for example, or some disagreement about a tax refund may involve only relatively small dollar amounts. Whether the amounts in controversy are large or small, Americans frequently feel compelled to pursue the matter even after they return to the States. The consulate can be of only limited help in these cases.

The State Department emphasizes that "the consular officer must make it clear that he/she cannot interfere with the administration of local laws, statutes or regulations." The consulate can, however, help you resolve the controversy informally by contacting the other party, relaying the claim, and determining whether the other party has any reasonable response, or interest in settling the matter.

In most cases the problem is usually a misunderstanding caused by distance and language differences, and the consulate can easily clear up the problem just by advising the parties of the confusion. And even when there is a real controversy between the parties, just the "inquiry" from the consulate may have enough moral force to break the deadlock.

In the last resort, if legal advice or litigation is warranted, the consulate will make its lawyers' list available. However, the consulate is not able legally to represent the interests of the American involved in civil claims abroad.

Medical Problems. Americans in Western Europe are no less susceptible to illness and accidents requiring medical attention than they are at home. Indeed, because of the rigors of travel —lost sleep, overexertion, exposure to differences in climate, anxiety, and anticipation—travelers suffer an increased risk of getting sick. If an American needs medical treatment for any reason, the consulate can be of some assistance.

First, and perhaps most important, an American in need of medical attention must find a competent, reliable, and English-speaking doctor. To that end, U.S. consulates generally maintain lists of local hospitals and English-speaking doctors. (For other information about finding a doctor in Western Europe, refer to the discussion in Section II: 5.) As with the list of lawyers, these medical lists vary in quality and helpfulness. The best lists contain enough background information (training, experience, specialties, etc.) to assist an American to make a reasonably informed choice about medical care. And, upon questioning, you may find that the consulate's list has been pruned to eliminate doctors whose competence is questionable. On the other hand, many consulates apparently give little attention to their medical lists, include only minimal information, and make no effort to monitor for quality.

Although the consulate staff is not permitted to recommend particular doctors (ostensibly because consular officials do not have the expertise to make such judgments, but more practically because the State Department does not want to be held responsible if anything goes wrong), many consular officials will be of assistance in directing you to the more well-regarded physicians. Rather than asking outright for a recommendation, you should try asking for the name of the doctor retained to treat the staff (many embassies and consulates retain the services of local physicians who may also be available for private patients), the name of the doctor used by local employees in the consular office, or the names of doctors who have been mentioned by other Americans as providing quality service.

Consulate officials are obviously reluctant to antagonize local authorities by criticizing the training or skills of local doctors. Therefore, consulates do not make a practice of offering judgments on a doctor's qualifications. On the other hand, proper medical care is too important to leave to random selection among unknown doctors identitied on a consulate list. Remaining sensitive to the consulate official's needs for discretion, you should nonetheless press for as much information as possible. Usually, upon inquiry (sometimes insistent inquiry), the consulate will confidentially reveal—"off-the-record," as it were—considerably more information than appears on the face of the medical list.

When an American becomes seriously ill—mentally or physically—while abroad, the consulate's capacity to help is limited, but not inconsequential. Note, however, that the United States will not pay for an American's medical care; each American must pay for such care as is required. Therefore, the most important medical advice for any American travelers is:

Make sure you have medical insurance. If you have insurance in the United States, make sure it applies abroad; if it does not, buy medical insurance for your trip. There is no excuse for any American to travel without insurance.

The consulate can provide some important practical assistance to the American with medical problems. In addition to making available its lists of doctors and hospitals, the consulate can help contact family and friends in the United States, it can facilitate the collection of relevant medical history and the transmission of that information to the attending physicians in Europe, and it can act as a conduit for the transmission of private funds from family and friends to the American in need.

In the event medical evacuation becomes necessary, the consulate can be extremely helpful in assisting with the necessary arrangements. Once again, however, the State Department will not pay for the trip home. Because evacuation can be extremely expensive, insurance that covers it is a must.

Death. The death of an American abroad is certainly a most traumatic experience for any companion of the deceased, as well as for helpless family and friends back in the States. Fortunately, in cases of death, the consulate staff is probably more helpful than in any other emergency situation.

The consulate will take care of virtually all practical arrangements, except for paying the expenses of transport, which the State Department cannot do. Among other things, the consulate will, if necessary:

- locate and notify the next of kin;
- assist with arrangements for burial in Europe or transport of the body to the United States, in accordance with the instructions of the legal representative;
- facilitate payment of local expenses and disposition of personal effects, all in accordance with instructions;
- coordinate the services of all local government medical authorities, transportation carriers, the funeral home chosen by the family, etc.

Of course, local laws and rules must be complied with, and frequently adherence to the law causes delays that the family finds almost intolerable. But though the consulate cannot break the law or ignore the red tape, at least it knows the rules and how best to cut through the red tape. In many countries these details would be insurmountable difficulties if left to the family in the United States.

Estates. When an American dies in a foreign country, a U.S. consular authority has legal responsibility for the estate if the deceased has no legal representative in that country. For example, if a woman dies while traveling alone as a tourist, and has no family in the foreign country when she dies, the consulate will assume responsibility for her estate. If, on the other hand, she were traveling with her husband, the husband would naturally be the legal representative. In either event, the law of the country where the death occurs governs and must be adhered to by all concerned.

The immediate legal problem raised by the death of an American abroad is the protection and distribution of the individual's personal effects and property. If necessary, the consular official will:

- take physical possession of all personal property of value, or make lists of property left in the custody of others such as police, hotels, etc.;
- assess the value of personal property and pay local debts to the extent that funds are available;
- dispose of the property as instructed by the deceased's legal representative;
- prepare a general accounting of the handling of the estate.

The State Department generally, and the local consulates in

particular, will also assist family and legal representatives in filing the necessary legal documents and complying with local legal requirements. As always, the consulate cannot provide legal advice, but in the event legal counseling of litigation becomes necessary the consulate will make its list of lawyers available.

Financial Assistance. Americans encountering financial difficulties abroad generally suffer one of two kinds of problems.

By far the most common problem involves those Americans who are not impoverished but who, because of loss or theft or other such unexpected occurrences, find themselves without any immediate available financial resources. The second category of problem involves the American who is destitute: that is, the person who does not have enough money—either in Europe or in the United States—to cover necessary living and travel expenses.

Once again, with only limited exceptions, the general rule is that the State Department will not pay expenses or lend money. Rather, the consulate will attempt to help the individual deal with the difficulty through private, nongovernmental resources. Thus, with respect to individuals in both categories of financial distress, the consulate will help locate family and friends willing and able to help. In addition, the State Department has established a special emergency program—Citizen Services Trust Fund—to facilitate the transfer of funds to an American in need.

Normally, the transfer of money from the United States to Europe must be routed through banks or through Western Union, but this commercial transfer often takes many days to complete. As an alternative, the State Department has instituted a special emergency fund that permits far quicker relief for the stranded American abroad. It works like this:

- A person in this country (the depositor) first has to get the money you need to the State Department, Citizen's Emergency Services, Washington, DC 20520. That can be accomplished in one of two ways:
  a money order can be brought or sent directly to the State Department; or a bank can wire the money to the State Department's account at American Security Bank, State Department Branch 20, Washington, DC 20520 (there is a $25 bank charge for this service).

- The depositor must also prepare, and include with the money sent to the State Department, a statement indicating the name and address of the depositor, the name of the American abroad to whom the money is to be sent, and the American embassy or consulate where the money will be picked up by the recipient.

- A $15 fee will be deducted from the total by the State Department for this service.

Once the State Department in Washington receives the money, it cables the appropriate consulate, which is then authorized to release that amount to the American abroad. This procedure avoids the time which would have been necessary to transfer the money.

In addition to helping the traveler in finding private resources, the consulate has some additional power to help the American suffering the short-term cash-flow problem as well as the American who is destitute.

The person temporarily destitute because of loss, theft, or other emergency needs money only until resources from home can be mobilized and forwarded. In such circumstances, the individual may receive a small loan for subsistence purposes until that money arrives.

When an American is destitute, and hasn't the resources either to remain in Europe or to return home, the consulate will make every effort to assist him or her in contacting family and friends in the United States who may be able to help. When all other possibilities have been exhausted, and as a last resort, the government may authorize a repatriation loan, which may be used only for direct travel from the place of receipt to the United States. No further European travel is permitted.

Furthermore, a repatriation loan must be approved at the State Department in Washington, so the process is both time-consuming and laden with bureaucratic complexity. Finally, if the loan is approved, the individual's passport will be marked to indicate that such a loan has been granted, and no further travel outside the United States will be permitted until the loan is repaid. Indeed, Congress recently authorized the State Department to revoke the passport of, or deny a passport to, anyone who does not repay a repatriation loan.

Child Custody Disputes. The dramatic increase in child-custody "kidnappings" in the United States—where a child-custody arrangement ordered by one state is defied by the noncustodial parent who takes the child, usually to a different state—occurs internationally as well. Typically, a noncustodial parent takes a child from the United States to a foreign country, or prevents the child from returning to the United States after a visit to the foreign country.

In most cases, the custodial parent seeking the return of a child to the United States faces serious legal and practical difficulties. Until recently, the mere fact that a U.S. court had issued a custody decree was not binding on foreign courts. Rather, the custody issue was reconsidered in foreign courts, and new custodial decisions were rendered based on the laws, practices, and attitudes of the foreign country in question. (Such local procedures may include a preference for the parent who is a national of that country, or a preference for a parent of a particular sex, even if that parent is the abductor and is violating a previously ordered U.S. custody decree.) In light of these legal difficulties, and in consideration of the practical and emotional difficulties connected with an international child-custody fight, every effort must be made to obtain a negotiated resolution of the problem. Assuming those efforts are unsuccessful, however, the only legal remedy available to the custodial parent has been litigation in the country where the abducted child is located. However, because of the seriousness of this problem, and the relative helplessness of the parent in the United States, the State Department has negotiated a treaty providing for the respect and enforcement of one country's custody decrees by the courts of another country to which the child has been abducted.

At the time of this writing, the Hague Convention on the Civil Aspects of International Child Abduction was finalized, but not yet adopted, by the United States. If it is signed by the President and approved by the Senate—as expected—the convention would then apply to international custody disputes between a parent in the United States and a parent in any other country that signs it. Most, if not all, Western European countries are likely to participate.

The convention provides that when a child is wrongfully removed or retained, and less than a year has elapsed since that unlawful removal or relocation, the authorities in the state where the child is held "shall order the return of the child forthwith." If more than a year has elapsed, the state where the child is held must also order the return of the child unless it determines that the child is now settled in the new environment.

In the context of child-custody disputes, the State Department acknowledges that "the amount and type of assistance which the department and its Foreign Service posts can offer is quite restricted." Generally, this means that the consulate may be able to do no more than:

- help a parent locate the child;
- provide information about the welfare of the child (the Privacy Act, which generally prohibits the dissemination of information about a person without that person's consent, nonetheless permits the release of information about a minor child to either parent, regardless of custody);
- provide general information about local child-custody laws and procedures;
- provide the legal list, if a lawyer must be consulted;
- report any abuse or neglect to local authorities;

- if the convention is adopted by both the United States and the state where the child is, the State Department will also be able to assist in implementing its terms and obtaining the return of the child pursuant to the procedures prescribed by the convention.

Bear in mind, however, that the State Department does not have the authority to return the child physically to the control of the parent with legal custody. The State Department has emphasized that it "cannot take custody of a child, force his/her return to the United States, or attempt to influence child custody proceedings in foreign courts. (Department officers) may not help a parent regain physical custody of a child illegally or by force or deception."

The convention, to the extent it is adopted by the United States and other governments, has the potential to alter dramatically the legal rights and remedies of the parents involved in an international child-custody dispute. However, it will undoubtedly take some time for the convention procedures to be ironed out and its legal mechanisms to begin working smoothly. Therefore, if you are involved in an international child-custody dispute, you should contact a knowledgeable lawyer, or the State Department, Office of Citizens Consular Services, to determine whether the convention applies to your case, and if so, how to implement its provisions.

Selective Service Registration. The Selective Service Act requirement that 18-year-old men register with the draft can be satisfied while abroad. The Presidential Proclamation reinstituting draft registration specifically provided that young men who are out of the country when they become obligated to register may do so at consulate offices or other designated overseas registrars.

General Information and Services. Because the mission of a consulate's Citizen Services Section is to help Americans abroad avoid difficulties, or help them deal with whatever difficulties may arise as capably as possible, a great deal of information and assistance is available to the traveler, beyond the subjects already discussed. In some matters, virtually all consulates can be of help; in others, a particular consulate may have prepared information about a matter arising frequently in the host country. For example, most consulates in Western Europe regularly maintain information about:

- doctors and hospitals
- attorneys
- local marriage requirements

- what to do if robbed
- while living in the country
  (for American residents).

Furthermore, all consulates offer a registration service, which permits Americans to leave their names and local addresses on file at the consulate in case of emergency. Registration is usually advisable only if the traveler intends to remain in one country for a significant period of time (or if the American will be traveling in areas of great danger, which is not usually the case in Western Europe).

The following are examples of country-specific information prepared by consulates to meet local needs:

- The consulate in Italy has a list of schools and universities in the country, because of the large number of Americans wanting to study there.

- The consulate in Greece has information about Greek currency restrictions, because the Greeks take those restrictions seriously. It also has compiled information about obtaining Greek public documents (such as birth and death records) because so many Greek-Americans want to search out their family histories.

- The consulate in Ireland has issued a travel advisory warning tourists about a sharp increase in local crime.

- The consulate in France has a special handout titled "Au Pair Employment in France," because so many young women seek such positions.

However, although the list of consular services is long, it is not endless. Almost every consular official I spoke with described one important limitation this way: the consulate is not a travel agency; it cannot help you find hotels, or book transportation, or recommend the sights. Nor is it a bank: it cannot cash your checks or make loans.

If you are in the United States and concerned about an American in trouble in Western Europe, you can contact:

Overseas Citizens Services
Department of State
Washington, DC 20520

Tel. (202) 632-5225 (8:15 *A.M.* to 10:00 *P.M.* Monday through Friday) and (202) 634-3600 (all other times, ask for Overseas Citizens Services duty officer). In addition, subject to the limitations of the Privacy Act, you may contact a consulate directly for information (see the country-by-country listings for addresses and telephone numbers).

II

TRAVELING IN WESTERN EUROPE

For most Americans, travel in Western Europe will be a joyous experience. The ethnic and physical diversity of the region can provide the makings of great adventure and yet the historical and cultural heritage we share with Western Europe make it comfortably familiar to Americans. As a result, Americans generally feel safer, more secure, in Western Europe than anyplace else in the world except home. It is easy, therefore, to let down our guard, to forget that international travel, even in Western Europe, is considerably more demanding than moving around in the States.

Nothing can poison a trip more than arriving to find the hotel does not have a room for you; losing your passport and money; getting in trouble with the law. The risks of such disruptions in Western Europe are considerably less than in many other places in the world, but even there successful travel requires some attention to details.

The discussions in this chapter, as well as in the country-by-country listings in the next, are intended to provide the framework for a safe and incident-free trip. And even when this book cannot provide the "answer," it will nonetheless alert you to the range of options available to you. By considering the legal and health concerns that confront the American traveler in Western Europe, you will be better prepared to avoid the pitfalls and to overcome any problems that arise.

---

1. CROSSING THE BORDER

All the countries of Western Europe can be reached from the United States by air (and many by sea, as well); and countries of the Continent have unlimited access to one another across their contiguous borders by train, bus, and car. Thus, there are many ways an American traveler may cross a border into a Western European country, and the potential difficulties and problems vary according to the circumstances. For the most part, however, the borders of Europe are wide open and easily crossed without formality.

■ ENTERING BY AIR

The common means of transportation from the United States to Western Europe today is by air. Therefore, American travelers find themselves going through immigration and customs at an airport in Western Europe at least twice: coming from, and returning to, the United States. Frequently, intra-European travel is done by air as well, particularly when the traveler's itinerary includes either the United Kingdom or Ireland in the northwest, or Greece in the southeast.

Generally, border-crossing procedures are the most formal, and most strict, at international airport arrival facilities. Of course, the rigor of the processing varies from place to place depending on many factors, such as the country's political and economic concerns, the precise regulations governing customs, and where the plane is coming from (passengers on flights from countries known for their illegal drug trade, for example, are more likely to be searched than passengers on flights from the United States). And, of course, recent concerns about terrorism and airplane hijacking have affected the intensity of security and customs processing throughout the world. However, other considerations aside, border-crossing formalities are likely to be more rigorous at airports than at other points of entry into the country.

To call these Western Europe border-crossing formalities strict, however, is only by way of comparing them to the procedures employed when entering a country by train or car. On the other hand, compared to the procedures necessary to enter the United States, the Western European formalities are rather modest and noticeably less burdensome.

Immigration. Virtually every Western European country requires that travelers pass through an immigration check immediately after deplaning. For tourists or business travelers not planning an extended stay, this process involves nothing more than a passport examination, to see that it is valid and that it belongs to the traveler presenting it.

- A valid U.S. passport generally permits entry into any Western European country for at least three months.

- An American without a valid passport may not enter any Western European country.

- Persons planning an extended stay in any Western European country must have the requisite visas and permits and present them for inspection and approval. (These are described in the country-by-country listings that follow in the next chapter.)
- The only significant problem regularly encountered at the immigration check is the long lines waiting to get through. For example, on a busy day at London's Heathrow Airport, in the midst of the tourist season, the delay may be considerably more than an hour.

Customs. After immigration is customs. Passengers go to the baggage claim area, collect all luggage, and then must decide whether to pass through the red-light or green-light customs stations. The red-light/green-light system, which is common throughout Western Europe, expedites the processing of travelers who have no dutiable or restricted items to declare. The system works like this:

- The customs regulations relevant to most travelers are usually (though not always) posted. More detailed information may be obtained in the country-by-country listings of this book, or by asking a customs official.
- If a traveler is carrying any dutiable or restricted items he or she must proceed to a red-light station. There an inspector will undertake whatever examination is necessary, make the appropriate assessments and determinations regarding entry, and grant the required authorizations once the formalities are completed.
- If a traveler is not carrying any dutiable or restricted items, he or she may proceed through the green-light station. Typically, the green-light traveler will pass directly through customs without further examination (unlike entering the United States, where even green-line passengers are individually examined by an inspector). There are customs inspectors watching the flow of traffic through the green-light station, and all travelers are subject to examination or search if the inspector thinks it appropriate. (In some places inspectors conduct routine spot checks on green-light passengers, so there is no reason to be concerned if stopped.)

Typically, a traveler found violating customs laws in Western Europe will not be treated harshly, as long as it appears that the violation was the result of a mistake, or that the goods in question were not meant for commercial use. Therefore, although some of the customs laws are confusing and complex, the average traveler needn't worry that a minor, inadvertent offense will result in being carted off to jail.

For example, a traveler caught carrying a few extra bottles of liquor and a few dollars' worth of souvenirs (assuming the quantity is not sufficient to raise suspicions of commercial dealing) will, at most, be required to pay a duty penalty amounting to two or three times what the normal duty would have been. Of course, the examination, the explanations, and the resolution might cause considerable delay, particularly if the traveler and the inspector have language difficulties, but no serious harm is likely.

However, if a traveler appears to be smuggling for purposes of business dealings, then the problem becomes more serious. These are hard economic times for Western Europeans, and any significant cheating at customs is treated as a serious matter. This is not to say, even then, that the traveler will be prosecuted, much less sent to jail. But it does generally result in the matter's being referred to a higher authority, which means even more delay, and the risk that the decision will be made on grounds that have little to do with a particular traveler—such as whether it is deemed necessary to set an example, the domestic political pressures on the officials involved, the state of the country's international affairs, and other concerns.

Finally, intentionally smuggling prohibited items—like drugs—is the most serious offense, particularly if there are indications of commercial activity. Among the items commonly prohibited or restricted throughout Western Europe are the following:

- weapons (other than for sport shooting, which must be declared in any event);
- materials that infringe local copyright laws;
- articles potentially carrying disease (thus, all plants and animals must be declared);
- currency and gold (depending on the country);
- illegal drugs (authorities are especially alert for the harder drugs, such as heroin and cocaine, because most countries are experiencing epidemiclike problems with them); note also that any narcotic drugs you need for medication should be carried in their original containers and, to play it safe, should also be accompanied by a doctor's certification attesting to the medicinal value of the prescription.

■ ENTERING BY SEA

Americans arriving in Western Europe aboard regularly scheduled passenger ships will dock at established port facilities and will be processed in essentially the same manner as airline passengers.

In some instances, typically in connection with cruises in the Mediterranean and Aegean seas, an American may enter Western Europe (Greece, for example) aboard a private ship or yacht. In such circumstances, the boat is supposed to make its first stop at a designated port of entry, where appropriate tourist documentation for the vessel, the crew, and the passengers may be obtained, and where the customs procedures are completed.

Barring any suspicions about the vessel's cargo, customs procedures are generally a mere formality.

■ ENTERING BY LAND

Land entry into the countries of Western Europe is usually the easiest of all. Intercontinental trains pass from one country to another with barely any indication of having crossed a border. Occasionally an official of the newly entered country will pass through the cars examining passports. A baggage check on the train is rarer still.

Automobile border crossings are also usually painless, although the traffic congestion can be a bit annoying.

Of course, regardless of the intensity of the customs check, incoming Americans are subject to all customs restrictions and controls. And customs officials have the power to enforce these rules and regulations, even if they have generally not done so in the past. So be careful.

---

2. MONEY AND BANKING

These days, "money" comes in many different forms: currency, credit cards, traveler's checks, personal checks, certified bank checks, etc. To best serve the average traveler's purposes, money should be readily negotiable, safe from loss or theft, and available as cheaply as possible.

Of course, no one form of money satisfies all those criteria. For example, local currency will be perfectly negotiable, but entirely unprotected if lost; contrarily, a cashier's check drawn on a U.S. bank may be fairly safe, but virtually unnegotiable. And traveler's checks may be generally negotiable and safe, but they do cost a fee to use.

The traveler must make a decision about which form of money, or which combination of forms, best serves his or her particular needs. Generally, a combination of forms is advisable.

■ TRAVELER'S CHECKS

Most knowledgeable travelers and travel advisers recommend

the use of traveler's checks. In Western Europe, traveler's checks can be readily exchanged at banks and other official exchange facilities (which usually offer the best exchange rates) , as well as at most restaurants, hotels, and shops catering to tourists (which frequently charge substantial service fees) . Except for small purchases, at exclusive restaurants, and in out-of-the-way places, traveler's checks are usually readily negotiable.

Traveler's checks are generally protected against loss and theft, if they have been signed by the traveler and the serial numbers have been recorded separately and can be reported to the company.

The only drawback to traveler's checks is that they usually do not come free (although the traveler should be alert to promotional offers from certain banks and automobile clubs) : usually traveler's checks cost 1 percent of their face value. Most travelers find that a small price to pay for the convenience and safety.

Traveler's checks are issued by, among others, American Express, Citibank, Bank of America, Barclays Bank and Thomas Cook Travel and are available throughout the United States at banks and other financial institutions.

■ FOREIGN CURRENCY

When dealing in foreign currency carry only as much as is consistent with immediate needs. Certainly, small amounts of foreign currency are needed to deal with tips, telephones, cabs, etc. But it is unwise to carry large amounts because other forms of currency—traveler's checks and credit cards, for example—are just about as negotiable and a lot safer.

Foreign currency can be obtained in a number of ways. First of all, dollars can be converted into local currency at most banks. (Interestingly, though, a dollar in cash is usually converted at a less favorable rate than the same amount in a traveler's check, the reason being the additional cost of security—currency has to be guarded more carefully than traveler's checks, which become functionally worthless after they have been countersigned.) In addition, as noted above, traveler's checks can be exchanged for foreign currency And a credit card can be used to obtain a cash advance from an institution honoring the particular card (subject, of course, to the credit restrictions of the card) .

Thus American Express offices will provide cash to American Express cardholders. And banks affiliated with Master-Card or Visa, including but not limited to branches of American banks in Western Europe, will give cash advances against those credit cards.

Lastly, Americans can purchase foreign currency for dollars

before leaving the United States. One of the largest currency dealers is Deak-Perera, headquartered at 29 Broadway, New York, NY 10006, with branch offices throughout the country. Deak-Perera sells foreign money by credit charge and can make arrangements to send you the foreign money by mail, if there is enough time before the travel begins. However, this option makes sense only if the travel is restricted to one country, and even then the traveler would be well advised to check currency import restrictions before making large purchases.

■ CREDIT CARDS

American Express, MasterCard, and Visa, along with many other major American credit cards, are widely accepted throughout Western Europe and generally provide good value. Unlike the fee charged for traveler's checks (and assuming the cardholder pays his bills on time) , no service charge is incurred for purchases made by credit card.

Furthermore, credit-card companies generally assess the exchange rate on the day the charge is posted to the account, not the day of the purchase. Thus, in times of a strong dollar, the rate may improve during that time resulting in savings for the traveler. (If the dollar exchange rate worsens between the date of purchase and the date of posting, the traveler will be charged the difference.) Travelers should list separately, and hold safe, the account numbers of all credit cards in case of loss. In addition, keep a record of the telephone number you should call to report the loss of the credit card, if that becomes necessary.

■ BANKS

Foreign banks will generally be of use to the average American traveler only to cash traveler's checks and provide credit-card cash advances. Generally, foreign banks will not permit any account transactions by nonresident travelers, and they will not cash a traveler's personal checks.

Moreover, although many American banks have branches throughout Western Europe, these foreign branches are almost always established for business transactions and often do not provide any personal banking services. Therefore, they are of as little use to the traveler as foreign banks. American bank branches affiliated with a credit card, however, will give a cash advance on that card.

The big question is whether foreign branches of American banks will cash the personal checks of travelers who have accounts with those banks in the States. The answer varies from bank to bank, and sometimes from branch to branch. (Therefore, if a traveler thinks he will be in need of this service, it would be advisable to check with his bank before leaving the United States.) However, even when the bank will cash a personal check, it will usually have a limit on the amount of cash available and require the traveler to wait up to two weeks while the check clears before the money is paid. Obviously, this is not a method of cash management that ought to be relied upon, although if all else fails it is certainly worth a try.

---

3. HEALTH

The two most important health-related pieces of advice for American travelers in Western Europe are: (1) have adequate medical and hospitalization insurance that applies outside the United States; (2) if possible, the coverage should include the costs of medical evacuation, should that become necessary.

■ INSURANCE

Many Western European countries have national health-care systems that provide excellent services to their own nationals, at little or no cost. While some countries used to make these services available to everyone—tourists and nationals alike — that is no longer the case. Thus, Americans abroad must be prepared to bear the expense of their own health care.

Of course, the countries of Western Europe operate public hospitals that provide services free of charge if the patient cannot pay. However, these facilities, particularly outside major metropolitan areas, are of uneven quality, and cannot be relied on to provide the level of care Americans customarily expect.

In the event the traveler's medical insurance does not cover treatment incurred abroad, or if the traveler is without medical insurance altogether, there are insurance companies that sell travel medical insurance plans at relatively low cost. The names and terms of these insurance policies can be obtained from an insurance broker or travel agent. In addition, companies providing these services frequently advertise in travel magazines and newspaper travel sections.

When traveling, be sure to carry your insurance information with you, including the name of the company, any applicable policy numbers, and a telephone number where service inquiries may be answered.

■ HEALTH CONCERNS IN WESTERN EUROPE

Travelers to Western Europe are usually casual about health-care concerns. To some extent, that nonchalance is justified. After all, Western Europe is environmentally much like the United States so that, with only a few exceptions, the American traveler's system is not subjected to dangerous water, food, or sanitation. And like the United States, Western Europe is free from serious contagious diseases. On the other hand, whereas a sense of ease about health matters is entirely justified, complete indifference to health-care, concerns is a big mistake.

First, the very act of traveling makes one increasingly susceptible to illness. As the World Health Organization points out:

> The majority of international travelers are subject to certain stresses that may lower resistance to disease. These include crowding, disruption of the usual eating and drinking patterns over quite long periods, and time changes with "jet lag" contributing to a disturbed pattern of the sleep and wakefulness cycle. These conditions of stress can themselves lead to nausea, indigestion, fatigue, or insomnia.

(The World Health Organization publication "Vaccination Certificate Requirements for International Travel and Health Advice to Travellers" may be obtained in the United States from: WHO Publications Center, 49 Sheridan Avenue, Albany, NY 12210; or the United Nations Bookshop, The United Nations, New York, NY 10017.) Second, although travelers to Western Europe will probably not encounter any major health threat of epidemic proportions, there are some health problems that, though not life threatening, could nonetheless ruin a perfectly good vacation. For the most part, such problems can be avoided entirely, or at least minimized, by the knowledgeable traveler.

Climatic Conditions. Travelers who fail to prepare for the climate of the locale being visited may not only ruin their trip but threaten their health as well. This is particularly true in the case of the elderly, who are especially susceptible to extremes of temperature, and temperature fluctuations.

In addition, a traveler's vacation activities—such as sightseeing—may themselves contribute to health problems. For example, the traveler in a hot, humid climate who exhausts himself checking out every point of interest may suffer salt and water deficiencies that could lead to serious dehydration, heat exhaustion, or worse.

Fortunately, information is available to help the traveler plan. wisely for the trip: the tourist information provided free of charge by every European country includes climate and other information helpful in planning a healthy trip; most guidebooks contain similar information regarding temperature and weather conditions at various times of the year, as well as advice about any special health problems; American consulates provide useful information about local climatic conditions.

Food and Water Conditions. For the most part, the food and water in Western Europe is as safe for Americans as food and water in this country. Of course, even in this country, when traveling to regions known for unusual foods and ingredients, the traveler is well advised to sample the fare in moderation; the same is true for travelers in Western Europe. However, in some circumstances, the food and water conditions can be a problem for Americans.

Throughout the south of Western Europe, particularly in the southeastern countries of Italy and Greece (as well as Yugoslavia) and the southwestern countries of Spain and Portugal, American travelers may be susceptible to a gastrointestinal infection causing severe diarrhea, especially during the hot summer months.

Although each person has a different tolerance for the bugs that cause this condition, the vast majority of American travelers remain perfectly happy and healthy in the major tourist areas and facilities (hotels, restaurants, etc.) . However, the likelihood of contracting the dreaded "runs" increases as the traveler moves away from the metropolitan centers into the countryside.

The bug causing the diarrhea enters the body in food and water. The World Health Organization advises all travelers as follows:

> *All raw food is liable to contamination and the traveler should avoid salads and uncooked vegetables and thin-skinned fruits. Undercooked and raw meat, fish and shellfish may also carry various intestinal pathogens.*

As local water sources may be contaminated as well, the U.S. Public Health Service recommends that travelers rely on:

- beverages made with boiled water, such as coffee or tea
- canned or bottled carbonated beverages, including carbonated water or soft drinks; beer and wine.

(The U.S. Public Health Service publishes "Health Information for International Travel," Government Printing Office No. CDC 84-8280. The Government Printing Office can be contacted at North Capital Street, Washington, DC, (202) 783-3238. Branch offices of the Public Health Services are maintained in most major cities.) A word of caution: Some travelers who scrupulously avoid drinking local water, nonetheless unthinkingly use ice made from the same water they are trying to avoid. Obviously, ice should be avoided as well. Furthermore, even an otherwise safe can of soda pop may have been cooled in that ice, thus contaminating the outside of the can itself and making drinking directly from it unsafe. Thoroughly drying the can should provide the necessary protection. And keep in mind that glasses and other containers that might have been used with the local water are also to be avoided unless thoroughly dried first, and preferably boiled.

Finally, a person planning to travel in high-risk areas should consider bringing along appropriate medication. Nonprescription medications, such as Pepto Bismol or Kaopectate are readily available at home but may be hard to come by in, say, the Spanish countryside. Furthermore, you may want to ask your doctor about the advisability of carrying one of the more powerful binding drugs, such as Lomotil, for emergencies.

Sexual Diseases. Anyone who has been awake for the last year must be aware that there is an epidemic of sexually transmitted diseases in this country. Although the problem does not seem to generate as much press attention in Western Europe as it does in the United States, contagious sexual diseases are a problem there as well.

Many travelers on vacation, or otherwise away from the constraints of their normal lives, are in the mood for sexual adventure in circumstances where sexual promiscuity is possible. And Western Europe offers no small number of willing partners, many of them professionals. The professionals, naturally, have a high rate of contact with venereal disease (although in countries where prostitution is controlled by the government, medical checkups and treatment are mandatory and the incidence of VD may be lower among professionals than among the general population).

There are no foolproof measures for avoiding contracting VD. The World Health Organization recommends: "The use of condoms by men and (though less effective) of emulsifying products by women, together with the thorough washing of the genitals after sexual intercourse, can go some way to providing protection."

Of course, suspicious symptoms should be checked by a physician immediately.

■ FINDING A DOCTOR

If a person does become ill while traveling in Western Europe, whether it is a minor affliction or a major illness, the most immediate concern is finding a reliable doctor with whom the traveler can communicate comfortably. The traveler will undoubtedly be concerned about the condition, whatever it is, anxious about getting sick in a foreign country, and in need of reassurance from the doctor, as well as good medical treatment. In short, this is not the time for the patient to be practicing a foreign language. If the traveler does not speak the native language fluently, it is important to find a capable English-speaking doctor. There are a number of ways of going about it.

First, American consulates maintain lists of the English-speaking doctors in their areas. Such lists can be extremely helpful, particularly if no other sources of information are available. But there are drawbacks.

For one thing, the consulate listing does not constitute a recommendation, and the consulate takes great pains to emphasize that it takes no responsibility for the qualifications or competence of the doctors on its list. With few exceptions, any doctor can get on the list just by making a request.

In addition, the lists vary in quality and comprehensiveness from place to place. Some consulates provide a great deal of helpful information about the doctors (age, training, experience). Many list specialists and provide several names to choose from. The lists prepared by other consulates are short and provide considerably less information, with few, if any, indications of specialties.

Another problem with the consulate's list is that the traveler will normally not have occasion to consider it until after the sickness sets in—which can be a problem if the illness is serious if the traveler is some distance from the consulate, or if the illness occurs on a weekend.

An alternative is to subscribe to a service that lists English-speaking doctors throughout Western Europe. The traveler can obtain the list before leaving the United States, take it on the trip, and have it available immediately in the event of medical emergency. Frequently, the service also includes a guarantee of maximum rates.

One such service is the International Association for Medical Assistance to Travelers (IAMAT), founded by Toronto physician Vincenzo Marcolongo. Members are provided, free of charge, with the following:

- a world directory of IAMAT physicians, including telephone numbers;
- a chart providing information about immunization and many of the most significant contagious diseases in over 200 countries around the world;
- world risk charts and related information about malaria and schistosomiasis;
- world climate charts, including information about seasonal clothing and sanitation. (Available only to members who make contributions.)

The IAMAT world directory only lists doctors who have satisfactory professional qualifications and have agreed to the following schedule of fees for IAMAT members:

- office visit, $20;
- house visit, $30;
- night visit, $35;
- weekend visit, $35.

Note, however, that referrals, consultations, laboratory procedures, hospitalization, and other medical services are not subject to the same fee schedule.

IAMAT can be contacted, and membership obtained, by writing to:

IAMAT
736 Center St.
Lewiston, NY 14092

Another service providing the names of English-speaking doctors is INTERMEDIC, Inc., 777 Third Ave., New York, NY 10017. Membership is $6 per year for an individual and $10 for a family, in consideration of which the member is entitled to:

- a worldwide listing of English-speaking doctors, with office and, frequently, home telephone numbers;
- make telephone inquiry to the INTERMEDIC central office about the data (medical education, experience, and hospital affiliation) on each doctor;
- make written inquiry to the INTERMEDIC central office about immunizations and medications advisable for the area of travel.

According to INTERMEDIC, "each INTERMEDIC physician has stated a willingness to respond promptly to calls from INTERMEDIC members." And they have also agreed to the following fee schedules: office visit, $30-$40; day house visit, $40-$50; night house visit, $50-$60. These fees are for the first visit only. Subsequent fees are subject to arrangement between the doctor and patient.

Another useful service for people suffering specific medical problems—anything from an allergy (e.g., to certain drugs) to a disease (e.g., diabetes or epilepsy) —is the medical tag provided by the Medic Alert Foundation. The tag contains the essential medical information, an identification number, and a toll-free telephone number that can be called in the event of a medical emergency. Medic Alert can be contacted at:

P.O. Box 1009
Turlock, CA 95381

840 North Lake Shore Drive
Chicago, IL 60611

777 United Nations Plaza
New York, NY 10017
tel. (1-800) 344-3226.

There is a charge for membership, but it varies depending on the type of tag chosen.

These are not the only health information services available to American travelers. Additional information may be obtained from your travel agent or through advertisements found in travel publications.

4. INTERNATIONAL DRIVER'S LICENSE

Although many Western Europe countries accept U.S. driver's licenses as valid, the American traveler would be well advised to obtain an international driver's license, which is valid for one year.

Even in countries where the U.S. license is accepted, driving on an American license may cause problems if the traveler is required to present it for any reason. For example, if an American tourist is stopped for a traffic violation in a rural area where English is not spoken, the police officer may not understand the U.S. license, may be annoyed by having to deal with it, and may cause difficulties for the traveler.

The international driver's license is printed in nine languages —including English, Spanish, Italian, German, and French— and is familiar to other drivers and the authorities throughout Western Europe.

The international driver's license is issued in this country by the Automobile Association of America (AAA) and can be obtained at most AAA offices or by writing to the AAA at Falls Church, Virginia 22047. To get an international driver's license, the traveler must:

- be 18 years old (even if the state of residence permits driving at a younger age);
- have a valid American driver's license;
- have two passport photographs;
- pay a $5 fee.

5. BREAKING THE LAW

Americans traveling in Western Europe (and throughout the world, for that matter) must understand one fundamental rule about the law: *Americans are always subject to the laws of the country in which they are traveling.*

It seems like such an obvious principle, but one too many Americans forget once they leave the United States. Americans in trouble with the law all too often assume that they will be able to "get off" just because they are citizens of the United States. It does not work that way.

In some parts of the world, the potential legal problems for the American traveler are compounded by the existence of laws or penalties not common in our country. For example, in some conservative Middle Eastern countries alcohol is prohibited and women are expected to dress with exceptional discretion; failure to abide by these restrictions can occasion some serious difficulties. Needless to say, ignorance of the law will not be much of a defense.

Fortunately for Americans traveling in Western Europe, however, variations in local law are rarely, if ever, so unusual that an American will get in trouble for doing things that would be legal in this country. Because the United States shares with the countries of Western Europe so many historical, cultural, social and political similarities, we tend to have a common understanding of what is right and wrong.

In short, the traveler can safely be guided by one general rule of thumb:

If it is illegal in the United States, it is likely to be illegal in the countries of Western Europe as well, and you probably should not do it. On the other hand, if it is legal in the United States, it is probably also legal in the countries of Western Europe.

Of course, we all know that, as a practical matter, not all crimes are enforced by the authorities with the same enthusiasm. In the United States each of us has a sense of what we can and cannot get away with in our own communities. It may not be right of us to break the law, but we know how much above the speed limit will be tolerated, and how many extra deductions can be safely claimed, and even how much marijuana can be purchased without serious concern about prosecution.

Needless to say, the authorities in the countries of Western Europe have their own enforcement priorities. Certain crimes—assault, rape, robbery and major money offenses—will be pursued vigorously everywhere. As to the lesser offenses, while it is fair to say that the same acts may generally be criminal in both the United States and Western Europe, it is not true that the authorities will treat the crimes the same.

In other words, just because you can get away with it in the United States does not mean you can also do it safely in Western Europe. The opposite is true as well. Drug offenses are a good example: In many parts of this country the police take seriously the possession of even small amounts of marijuana, while in the Netherlands, for example, the same offense would be ignored by the police. Conversely, a drug violation that would be treatad with relative indifference by the Los Angeles police might be dealt with considerably more harshly in many cantons of Switzerland.

It is important, therefore, not to assume that minor infractions of the law can be committed in the countries of Western Europe just because you may engage in the same conduct with impunity in the United States. Regrettably, there is no workable formula for determining local enforcement priorities; not only do they differ from country to country, they vary from place to place within each country (which is true in our country as well).

For the cautious traveler, therefore, the best advice is to stay well within conservative standards of conduct, and it is extremely unlikely you will encounter any difficulties with the law. For the incautious traveler, no advice will do anyway, but I do have a few personal observations that may be relevant to the severity with which your conduct is judged.

First, Western Europeans have a much more developed sense of propriety than is now in vogue in the United States, particularly with respect to the integrity of the individual. As a result, criminal acts likely to hurt another person seem to be more offensive in Western Europe than in many places in the United States. For example, drunk driving in Europe has long been viewed with a severity that has only in recent years become common in this country. On the other hand, that same basically conservative respect for individual integrity leads many Western Europeans to treat the so-called victimless crimes—such as sexual offenses and drug use—less harshly than middle Americans might.

Second, all other things being equal, Americans involved with the law in Western Europe are likely to be treated better than other nationals because they are Americans. Of course, all things are rarely equal, and this observation is subject to wide variation depending upon such circumstances as whether the American is particularly obnoxious, what the international political climate is like at the moment, or the temperament of the government official involved. But in recent years, Western Europe seems to have gotten over the virulent anti-Americanism that dated back at least as far as the Vietnam era. These days Americans in Western Europe are treated, if not always as friends, at least as welcome visitors. Thus, assuming no major violation of public order or safety, an American caught breaking the law in some minor way—driving violations, for example, or even disregarding customs restrictions or currency regulations—will more likely than not be given the benefit of the doubt.

Third, the urban/rural distinctions that mark differing law-enforcement attitudes in this country seem to play out in similar ways in Western Europe. Simply put, the authorities tend to be more permissive in the cities than in the countryside, particularly with respect to the "morality" issues: drugs, sex, and rock and roll. In other words, if you have to let loose, downtown is safer than small town.

■ AMERICANS IN TROUBLE WITH THE LAW

Whatever Americans do in the United States, they do in Western Europe as well. Of course, there are a lot fewer Americans doing it in Western Europe, but at least one knowledgeable consular official guessed that the proportions were about the same. Thus, for example, Americans are regularly involved in motor vehicle incidents, bar brawls, and minor thefts like small-time shoplifting, as well as the more serious drug offenses and crimes of violence.

Most of the crimes committed by Americans in Western Europe are common offenses and do not warrant special discussion. Nor are there peculiarities of Western European law relating to these offenses that need special note. More than any other single factor, the severity of the crime will determine the authorities' response, and that response will result in an American's imprisonment only in extreme cases. However, there are a few particular legal problems deserving of attention here.

Illegal Drugs. The U.S. State Department puts out a brochure titled "Travel Warning on Drugs Abroad." Its message is this:

> From Asia to Africa, Europe to South America, Americans are finding out the hard way that drug possession or trafficking equals jail in foreign countries....DON'T LET YOUR TRIP ABROAD BECOME A NIGHTMARE!

The advice is clear and correct: Do not travel with illegal drugs, and do not try to purchase or use illegal drugs abroad.

- An American traveling in a foreign country does not have the "constitutional" protections he would enjoy in this country.
- Foreign customs and police officials have extensive powers to search for drugs and investigate suspected drug crimes.
- If caught, the American far from home is especially vulnerable to the peculiarities of local police practices and criminal law procedures. (The characteristics of Western European criminal justice systems are described later in this chapter and in the country-by-country listings.)

Without in any way mitigating the State Department's advice, the fact is that the consequences of a drug offense are worse in some parts of the world than in others, and for an American are probably less threatening in Western Europe than elsewhere. Of course, even focusing on just Western Europe, generalities are unreliable because:

- The type and quantity of the illegal drug involved will affect the severity of the government's response. It is fair to say that soft drugs (marijuana and hashish) will be dealt with less severely than hard drugs (heroin and cocaine), and small amounts will be dealt with less severely than large amounts.

- There are wide variations in attitude from country to country within Western Europe. For example, Amsterdam has a reputation for being permissive, at least with respect to the soft drugs, whereas even in the nearby cities of Germany drug offenses are treated more sternly.

- The consequences of a drug offense are often subject to the personal eccentricities of the particular official involved. Even where there is an informal policy of leniency, for example, a police officer may make a major case out of an otherwise minor drug offense simply because he needs to make an arrest that day, or because the individual offended him in some way.

With those cautionary limitations in mind, however, there are a few facts and observations about the drug scene in Western Europe that may be enlightening.

Technically, in most countries of Western Europe even small-scale, soft-drug possession and use are illegal. Moreover, in every country of Western Europe, trafficking in a controlled drug (which often means no more than the transfer of the drug from one person to another, even without payment) is definitely illegal.

Yet despite the seemingly strict criminal provisions throughout Western Europe, as of the end of 1984 there were only a handful of Americans imprisoned in Western Europe on drug offenses, and all of those cases involved significant trafficking in hard drugs. There were no Americans imprisoned in Western Europe merely for personal possession or use offenses. In other words, criminal prosecution leading to incarceration seems to be limited to people engaged in heavy trafficking in hard drugs. American tourists who have and use drugs for personal social purposes are not as a rule targeted for prosecution.

Of course, to say that Americans are not arrested and incarcerated for drug offenses does not mean that they suffer no consequences at all. If an American is caught—at an airport customs inspection, for example—with illegal drugs, something like the following can be expected: the American will be escorted from the customs area to a private interrogation room, where a determination will be made as to whether the drugs are for personal use. If such a determination is made, it is almost certain that no formal criminal proceedings will be instituted, but the drugs in question will certainly be confiscated.

If the American is deemed to be carrying drugs in excess of amounts likely to be for personal use, then more serious consequences may follow: heavy fines, deportation, or jail.

Sexual Matters. Despite the typical American's view of Western Europeans as staid and conservative, there exists a fairly consistent attitude throughout the Continent that private, consensual sexual conduct is a personal matter not subject to government control.

Prostitution. Prostitution is legal throughout most of Western Europe. By that I mean that exchange of sexual favor for money is not a crime. However, in almost all countries, the *business aspects* of prostitution are illegal. Thus, it is illegal for a man to pimp for a prostitute, for a woman to solicit customers for prostitution, or to run a house of prostitution. Of course, it does not take much effort to discover, particularly in the major tourist cities of Western Europe, that these laws are more honored in the breach than in the observance.

In any event, even when the police try to enforce the law, the customer   that is, the American traveler—is almost never involved. (Except for my general distrust of the absolute, particularly with respect to legal matters, I would have said that the customer is "never" involved. Suffice it to say that of the consular officials and local lawyers I interviewed throughout Western Europe, not one knew of a single instance in which an American traveler got into any legal trouble because of engaging the services of a prostitute.) Not surprisingly, just about every major city in Western Europe catering to tourists has its red-light district. Some of the more infamous, such as in Paris and Amsterdam, are almost tourist attractions and their locations are frequently noted in guidebooks.

Homosexuality. Homosexuality is accepted throughout Western Europe in much the same way it is in the United States. In most urban areas, gays and lesbians go about the city openly without any obvious harassment or interference. That surface acceptance means that gay or lesbian American travelers generally do not encounter any significant difficulties because of their sexual preferences. Undoubtedly, the more rural the area, the more likely it is to find expressed hostility to homosexuals, although probably less so in the countrysides of Western Europe than in the same areas in the United States.

On the other hand, homosexuals in Western Europe, as in

this country, often complain of the same deep-rooted institutional prejudice affecting their legal status at work, in the family, and in the community. For homosexual American travelers, however, whose visits may be sufficiently brief and superficial to avoid those underlying difficulties, the trip to Western Europe may provide a happy respite from the similar prejudices that await them on return to this country.

Pornography. Pornography in Western Europe has long since outstripped the now quaint "dirty" postcards sold in Paris, on the Left Bank. These days, hard-core pornographic materials may be obtained without much difficulty throughout Western Europe. In some places, the public display of pornography, such as at newsstands and shop windows, must be discrete—which usually means thin strips of tape over the pertinent body parts —but just about every city in Western Europe has its sex-shop district where pornography and sexual paraphernalia are freely available.

■ TOURIST OFFENSES

Many of the countries of Western Europe impose certain restrictions on American tourists ranging from traveler registration requirements to currency regulations and length-of-stay limitations (these restrictions are identified in the country-by-country listings). As with all legal restrictions, generalizations about enforcement are necessarily inaccurate because practices vary widely from place to place. Therefore, the American would be well advised to comply with these restrictions, particularly since they are rarely much of a bother anyway. With that admonition in mind, the following general observations seem warranted:

Of all the restrictions grouped under the heading "tourist offenses," the currency regulations are generally the most rigorously enforced. These regulations have been imposed to protect local currency in hard economic times, and are often taken very seriously by local authorities.

Of course, currency restrictions are not primarily aimed at tourists; the governments that impose currency control will not sink into bankruptcy because a few tourists exceed the applicable limitations. However, in their effort to stop others from violating the currency restrictions—their own nationals, for example—they will also take action against American travelers discovered in violation of the limits. If the point of rigorous enforcement is to "send the message" that the currency restrictions are meant to be taken seriously, then catching an American serves the purpose as well as catching anyone else.

However, an American would have to be involved in a serious violation before suffering significant consequences. A person caught in the business of black-market currency operations, or who was involved in a currency smuggling scheme, would undoubtedly be held, questioned extensively, and bound over for criminal prosecution. That person had better get a good lawyer.

On the other hand, the average American traveler who violates the applicable regulations—whether innocently, by not knowing what they are, or negligently, by not paying attention to them—will probably not suffer any consequences at all; at most he may be fined. Keep in mind that there are two kinds of currency limitations: restrictions on bringing money into the country, and restrictions on taking money out.

As a practical matter, the restrictions on taking money out of the country are the most important. However, customs formalities are typically far less rigorous leaving the country than entering (although keep in mind that the power of customs authorities to search you and your baggage upon departure is no less than upon entry). It would be extremely rare for foreign customs officials to check an American's wallet, purse, and pockets (which is where money would normally be kept) upon departure unless they already suspected a violation. Finally, an American traveling with a large amount of cash can usually avoid departure problems by declaring it upon entry.

Most of the other tourist restrictions described in the country-by-country listings—such as tourist registration requirements and length-of-stay limitations—should be adhered to by the American traveler. However, the violation of these restrictions in the countries of Western Europe will amost certainly not result in any criminal penalties. In some cases, a violation may cause some hassle for the traveler—questioning by the authorities, for example, along with the resulting delay—and, more rarely, the imposition of a fine. You should remember, however, that although the consequences may not be severe in any objective sense, even relatively minor hassles by the authorities can be sufficiently inconvenient to sour a good day. The more prudent course is to obey the law, particularly since it is so easy to do so.

■ SUFFERING THE CONSEQUENCES

Clearly, being "in trouble with the law" does not necessarily mean being thrown in jail, or even arrested (any more than it does in this country).

In 1984, for example, the State Department was notified that 510 Americans had been arrested in the countries of Western Europe. Between a third and a half of those arrests were for drug offenses, and the rest for crimes such as fraud, theft, drunk and disorderly conduct, assault, and weapons offenses.

Most experts believe, however, that the State Department figures underestimate the number of arrests because not all arrests of Americans are reported to the consulates. It is estimated that many more Americans were arrested for relatively minor infractions that were quickly resolved and not formally reported to the U.S. government. And, of course, even more Americans had some difficulty with the police, but were not arrested at all.

For the most part, Americans in trouble with the law are usually involved in minor offenses that do not result in imprisonment. Typically, an incident, such as a bar brawl or a vehicle violation, will be investigated by the police, the American will be questioned, forms will have to be completed and, ultimately, the matter will be dropped.

Infrequently, the preliminary proceedings will be followed by the American's arrest, the imposition of a fine, and, occasionally, a "request" that the individual leave the country.

Make no mistake about it, however, even without a jail sentence, the whole affair can be unpleasant enough to ruin your trip. It may also take a considerable amount of time to resolve and, especially if a lawyer has to be hired and/or a fine paid, the experience can be expensive.

Of course, some offenses are sufficiently serious to warrant an arrest and full criminal proceedings. As of the end of 1984, for example, the State Department reported that 324 Americans were imprisoned in Western Europe. Those cases—in which the American defendant is subject to the local criminal procedures—are considered next.

6. CRIMINAL PROCEDURES IN WESTERN EUROPE

Just as Americans are subject to the criminal laws of the country in which they are traveling, they are also subject to the same rules of criminal procedure applicable in that country. In other words, an American in trouble with the authorities in a Western European country will receive the same treatment accorded a national of that country—no better, no worse.

The difficulty for many Americans is that we tend to think of the "rights" we have in this country—the right to counsel, the right to make a phone call, the right to bail, the right to a jury trial, etc.—as fundamental. And we assume that those minimum protections will be provided to us wherever we are; particularly in the "civilized" countries of Western Europe. If you think that, you are wrong.

The central theme sounded by virtually every person interviewed for this book was this:

The Bill of Rights does not protect an American arrested in a foreign country. Whatever "rights" that country provides for its own nationals should be provided to the American;

if a right is not provided to nationals, the American will not receive it either. And though the U.S. consulate can try to ensure that Americans receive equal treatment, the consulate cannot obtain favored treatment for Americans.

Many Americans in trouble with the law abroad find that very hard to take, because the criminal justice systems throughout most of Western Europe are markedly different from ours. Particularly in the Continental countries, the law has evolved through historical and social circumstances different from those in the United States, and it is not surprising that those countries have developed many different mechanisms for determining criminal responsibility. This is not to say that there are not also many similar protections afforded to criminal suspects. For example, in all countries of Western Europe the accused has a right to counsel and the right to remain silent.

However, many of those common rights may, as a practical matter, be applied differently than they are in this country, thus seeming to diminish their impact. And frequently, the Western European legal systems do not provide at all for some legal safeguards we Americans have come to expect, such as jury trials.

As a result, the Western European systems of criminal procedure may occasionally seem downright unfair. Unfortunately, the American has no choice but to endure it; the foreign system will apply to the American, like it or not.

There may be an exception to that general rule, however: a legal system may be so unfair, or so offend accepted standards of conduct, that to apply its procedures to an American visitor would constitute a violation of accepted international human rights agreements. In such circumstances the American consulate can complain and, hopefully, obtain treatment for the American that at least satisfies minimum human rights standards. However, because the accepted standards of fairness and conduct are so broadly interpreted, it is clear that most aspects of the Western European criminal systems are well within those accepted limits. In the remainder of the discussion of Western European criminal legal systems I will assume that the law is not being applied in a way that violates international human rights, although such a claim may certainly be asserted if circumstances warrant.

The following description of what is likely to happen to an American caught up in criminal justice systems of Western Europe is designed to provide only a general overview of the procedures that will apply. The focus will be on the common attributes of the various systems of justice, rather than the specific details of each. Obviously, even among those countries whose systems derive from the same traditions, there will be variations in detail from place to place (just as in the United States, for example, the various state systems derive from a common legal heritage, but nonetheless have different rules and regulations). Therefore, anyone who is arrested, or is otherwise implicated in criminal justice matters in Western Europe, must consult an attorney expert in local law. The nearest American consulate will provide you with a list of English-speaking lawyers from which to choose.

■ COMMON LAW AND CIVIL LAW

The legal systems of Western Europe can be broadly categorized into two groups: "common law" systems and "civil law" systems. Both names refer to the historical legal tradition from which the system derives.

The "common law" countries of Western Europe are the United Kingdom and Ireland. The United States is also considered a common law country (except for Louisiana, with its strong French background). Because of our shared heritage with the English common law system, the criminal law procedures in the common law countries are most like our own.

The "civil law" countries of Western Europe are the ones that trace their legal history to the comprehensive written Codes of Law developed by a number of the Continental countries. The French Napoleonic Code is the most well known, though it was preceded by the Germanic codes and the ancient Roman Code of the Emperor Justinian. All of the Continental countries of Europe—that is, all the countries covered by this book, except the United Kingdom and Ireland—are civil law countries. Because these countries far outnumber the common law countries in Western Europe, and because the civil law system is very different from our own, the civil law system will be emphasized in the following description of criminal procedure in Western Europe.

■ ARREST

Assuming the police have sufficient reason to believe you are involved in a crime serious enough to take you into custody, you will be arrested—which is a process that is about the same everywhere. The rules governing the police power to make an arrest—whether the police need a warrant, when an arrest can be made without a warrant, etc.—vary from country to country. However, because the suspect is generally unaware of the impending arrest before it happens, there is very little the suspect can do to influence the manner in which the arrest is made. If the arrest is made illegally, that claim will have to be raised by the lawyer at a later stage of the proceedings. (Keep in mind, however, that such procedural irregularities are rarely treated as seriously as they are in the States.)

In most countries—both common and civil law — the police are required to bring the arrested suspect before a Magistrate as soon as practicable after arrest, usually within a day or two (though occasionally, as long as a week). During that period prior to the court appearance, while the suspect is in police detention, the authorities will likely conduct a lineup, if necessary, collect evidence, interview witnesses, interrogate the suspect and do whatever else is necessary to investigate the charges.

The rights of the inidividual at this stage vary from place to place, depending on both the terms of the law and actual police practices. However, although not too many generalizations are accurate, it is fair to say that an American will not likely enjoy as many rights in any other country as are afforded criminal suspects in the United States. For example, the suspect is often not allowed the expected one phone call. Indeed, sometimes the prisoner does not even have the right to see anyone, not even an attorney, until after some initial period of investigation. And even where the right to see an attorney exists, the police may be authorized to "delay" notification if necessary for police purposes. (In the United States, by contrast, if a prisoner requests counsel, the prisoner may not be held incommunicado for any period of time for questioning by the police.)

Keep in mind that anything incriminating the prisoner says can, and no doubt will, be used as evidence. (That friendly fellow prisoner in your cell may be a government plant, or may be willing to sell you out for the right price, so keep your mouth shut.) On the other hand, in every country a criminal suspect has the right to remain silent (although that right is often not explained to the prisoner, or it is communicated in a way that is not clear, for example by reciting a statement of rights quickly and in the local language to an American who speaks only English). Therefore, if you find yourself in these circumstances, the best advice is to try saying as little as possible until you have spoken with someone you trust, such as your lawyer or the American Consul. Every arrested American has the right to have the United States consulate informed of the arrest "without delay" and to visit with a consular official as soon thereafter as possible. This requirement is imposed by Article 36 of the Vienna Consular Convention, signed by the United States and every country of Western Europe (with the exception of the Netherlands, which is nonetheless bound to the same rules by operation of other treaties). It thus applies to every country of Western Europe, regardless of the legal system in place.

In most countries, particularly in the major metropolitan centers where the police have experience dealing with the arrest of travelers, notification usually occurs expeditiously and the consular visit to the arrested American can take place within the first day or two. If the American is arrested out in the countryside, however, the police may not move as quickly, they may not be as familiar with the applicable treaty requirements (remind them if need be) and the word may not get to the consulate for days. And then, of course, the consular official may not be able to travel to the place of arrest immediately.

Whenever that consular visit occurs, the consular official will: provide a list of local English-speaking attorneys, describe generally how the case will proceed (though the consular official cannot represent the American prisoner), convey information to family and friends (but only if you want them to know), and protest any mistreatment or abuse. (The role of the consular official following the arrest of an American is described in greater detail in Chapter 1.)

■ PRELIMINARY HEARING

Typically, after the initial police investigation, the case is referred to a prosecutor to determine whether there is sufficient reason for the case to go forward. Although the procedures differ from country to country, after some examination of the evidence the prosecutor usually has the power either to prosecute the case or dispose of it summarily without prosecution. If the decision is to prosecute the case, the prisoner will then have to be brought before a court. And at that point, the common law and civil law systems begin to differ dramatically.

In the common law countries, the prisoner will appear before a court official typically known as a Magistrate. The Magistrate is like a junior judge. The Magistrate has the power to issue arrest warrants, issue search warrants and summon witnesses. Most importantly for the prisoner in police detention, the Magistrate will also preside over a preliminary inquiry — a hearing of some sort, at which the prisoner and lawyers are present and permitted to offer witnesses and argument. The Magistrate then determines if there is enough evidence to commit the prisoner for trial. And if trial is ordered, the Magistrate will determine if the prisoner may be released from custody while awaiting trial.

In the civil law system, the investigative stage of the case is controlled by a "Judge of Instruction" (occasionally also referred to as the "Examining Magistrate") — a role that has no exact counterpart in our system.

In some respects the Judge of Instruction acts similarly to the common law Magistrate: typically, the Judge of Instruction decides whether the government has enough evidence to justify sending the case to trial or whether it should be dismissed;

and if the case is sent to trial, the Judge of Instruction decides whether the prisoner should be held in custody during the investigation or released awaiting trial.

The Judge of Instruction also acts in some respects similarly to a the common law prosecutor (and it is this aspect of the instructing judge's responsibilities that often seems unusual to Americans) . If the case is deemed sufficiently serious to deserve a trial, the Judge of Instruction actually conducts the formal investigation and assembles the file for the trial court. Thus, the Judge of Instruction will take statements from the defendant and all of the witnesses, collect all of the documentary evidence, obtain opinions from experts if necessary and conduct whatever other investigation is necessary to prepare the case for trial.

During this investigative stage, the defense counsel typically has little, if any, substantive involvement in the proceedings. The defense counsel may suggest that the Judge of Instruction question certain witnesses or pursue certain lines of inquiry. But the defense counsel is generally not allowed to be present during the examination of witnesses and frequently cannot even see the file compiled by the Judge of Instruction until the investigation is complete and the case is referred to trial.

In the common law countries, the pre-trial investigative stage proceeds very much like in the United States. The case is investigated by the police and prosecuted by a prosecuting solicitor. The defense counsel works independently to prepare the case for the defendant.

■ PRE-TRIAL CONFINEMENT AND BAIL

After a person has been arrested, and the judge of instruction concludes that there is sufficient evidence to warrant an investigation for trial, the court must also determine whether the suspect should be held in detention during the period of investigation and trial.

In the United States, we make the decision about pretrial confinement based on the application of a number of general principles:

- Because a person is always presumed innocent until after proven guilty, a criminal suspect has a right to be released awaiting trial.
- The only exception to the right of release arises if the defendant is likely not to return for trial.
- Therefore, we rely on a system of bail — an arrangement in which a defendant is released from pre-trial custody in exchange for posting a money bond as security to guarantee an appearance at trial.

- Bail is supposed to be set just high enough to assure the defendant's return, without being so high as to absolutely preclude release.
- Furthermore, because of our respect for the presumption of innocence, we generally do not permit preventive detention—that is, keeping prisoners in detention to prevent them from committing future crimes.

By comparison, pre-trial detention decisions in most other countries, including both common law and civil law countries, are based on the application of very different underlying presumptions and principles. In general:

- Defendants do not have any "right" to be free awaiting trial. The decision to free a prisoner is solely a matter of grace (although the individual court decisions may be appealed, if the Magistrate or Judge of Instruction does not follow applicable standards).
- The general rule is, nonetheless, to release defendants from custody while awaiting trial. However, the defendant is usually freed on provisional liberty—that is, on the defendant's own recognizance—without any bail at all. Western Europeans seem to rely on the rather quaint notion that when defendants are deemed trustworthy enough to be released, it is expected that they will live up to that trust and return for trial. And they usually do.
- Bail is extremely uncommon in Western Europe; it is seen as a discrimination against the poor. If a person is considered deserving provisional liberty it will be granted without bail, and if provisional liberty is not considered appropriate then it will generally not be granted despite an individual's ability to pay bail.
- Provisional liberty will be denied, however, if the court determines that there are reasons to believe any one of the following conditions exists:

  that the defendant will not appear for trial; or that the defendant will commit other crimes while free; or that the defendant may interfere with the prosecution of the case (such as by tampering with the evidence).

- Note that the last two of those three reasons for denying provisional liberty pertain to the prevention of the defendant's future crimes — in other words, unlike the general rule in this country, the Western Europeans do not prohibit preventive detention.

For Americans prisoners, these standards are usually very problematic. First, pretrial release is rarely provided anyone accused of a serious crime, such as drug offenses, because the likelihood that the defendant will not appear for trial, and the motivation to interfere with the prosecution, are substantial. Since Americans are usually only imprisoned for serious offenses, release is difficult to obtain. Furthermore, the very fact that an American is a foreigner increases the liklihood of non-appearance at trial, and makes it correspondingly more difficult to convince a court to permit pre-trial release from custody.

Fortunately, although bail is not common, it is not unheard of either, particularly for foreigners, and may be one of a number of techniques the court could use to assure that the American will not flee. Obviously, an American in this predicament must discuss these alternatives with counsel.

Assuming the American is kept in pre-trial detention, the length of that imprisonment can be substantial. In many countries, the permissible pre-trial confinement may extend for quite a few months and, on rare occasions even years. Generally, this pre-trial time is creditied to the sentence if the defendant is convicted; but it is a complete loss if the case ends in acquittal.

■ DEFENSE COUNSEL

In every country of Western Europe a defendant is entitled to legal counsel, and counsel will be appointed if the defendant cannot afford to retain one privately. The Western European countries do not generally have a public defender or legal aid program as such, but instead have adopted various arrangements for requiring the private bar to provide representation for the poor.

Thus all of the Western European countries, like the United States, respect the right to counsel. However, the role of defense counsel in Western Europe is very different from what we expect of counsel in the United States.

Particularly in the civil law countries, the defense counsel seem to have a very passive involvement in the proceedings: they frequently are not permitted even to meet with the client until many days after the investigation has begun, and after the client has been interrogated by the police; they are restrained from actively investigating the case the way an American lawyer would because that responsibility resides with the Judge of Instruction; and they are usually not even allowed to attend the pre-trial examination of witnesses by the Judge of Instruction, much less cross-examine those witnesses.

Furthermore, once the trial begins, defense counsel does not engage in the vigorous argument, presentation of evidence and cross examination so common in American courtrooms. As described below, the trial is usually quite subdued by American standards, with great reliance placed on the investigative file prepared by the Judge of Instruction during the investigative phase.

In the common law countries of the United Kingdom and Ireland, the lawyer's role in the criminal justice system will appear much more familiar to the American. One big difference distinguishing the United States is that in the United Kingdom, and most other common law countries, the attorney's job is split between two kinds of lawyer: the solicitor and the barrister. The solicitor generally interacts with the client, providing legal advice and assistance in matters outside of the actual courtroom, and the barrister is hired by the solicitor to argue the client's case in court.

■ THE PLEA BARGAIN

Plea bargaining — the process whereby the prosecution and the defense negotiate a settlement to a criminal case that usually results in the defendant's pleading guilty, but to a lesser crime than originally charged—is virtually unheard of in the Western European systems of criminal justice.

■ TRIAL

A criminal trial in a civil law court is likely to be very unnerving to any American expecting a "Perry Mason" drama.

First, many civil law countries do not use juries at all. And even the countries that do, provide juries only for trial of the most serious offenses, such as murder. Therefore, the vast majority of defendants are tried before one or a number of judges (depending on the seriousness of the charges) sitting without a jury.

Second, the judge, rather than the lawyers, actually conducts the trial. In other words, the judge, not the lawyers, calls the witnesses and asks the questions. After the judge finishes questioning the witness, the judge may allow the lawyers to ask a few questions:, but rigorous cross examination of the sort common in American courtrooms is out of the question.

Although the judges and lawyers are often clothed with the trappings of formality, the proceedings are usually conducted with a chatty informality, and without any apparent regard for strict rules of evidence. The judge will also likely rely heavily on the file prepared by the Judge of Instruction, and may not even call a witness if the statement in the file is clear and essentially uncontested.

Lastly, unlike any procedure known in American criminal law, the victim of the crime (if there is a specific victim) may also be represented by counsel at the trial and may participate in the proceedings. And if the defendant is found guilty, one aspect of the sentence may include restitution to the victim.

After the trial is completed, the judge will usually render a decision quickly, often right on the spot. That decision will include both a determination of guilt or innocence and, if guilty, the sentence imposed on the defendant.

A trial in the United Kingdom and Ireland may look a lot different from an American trial—what with all the pomp and circumstance of the British courtroom—but procedurally it will be more similar to the American system than a civil law trial. However, even in these common law countries, the trial will almost always be conducted with "gentlemanly" restraint and, for the American, will be marked by a distinct lack of the aggressively active lawyering that we have come to expect of lawyers in this country.

Assuming the crime charged is sufficiently serious, it will be tried in the Crown Court, before a jury and with a full adversary proceeding in which the lawyers take the lead in the presentation of the case. After being instructed in the law, the jurors will decide the guilt or innocence of the defendant.

■ APPEAL

Both the common law and civil law systems provide for an appeal if the defendant is found guilty. The precise procedures applicable to the appeal, however, always vary from country to country.

Although those procedural details involve complex legal technicalities, they may also have some very significant consequences for the defendant.

For example, in many civil law countries both the defendant and the prosecutor may appeal from an adverse decision. In other words, if you are found not guilty by the trial judge the prosecutor may appeal seeking to have the appellate court find you guilty; and if you were found guilty but given little or no punishment, the prosecutor may ask the appeals court to increase your sentence.

In the common law countries, including the United States, the prosecutor usually has no right to appeal a jury verdict finding the defendant not guilty, and no right to seek a higher sentence on appeal.

Another important question involves the scope of the appeal; that is, whether the appellate court may review only disputed legal issues, or disputed factual questions as well. In civil law countries, there is typically one appeal permitted of both legal and factual questions. However, in common law countries, the general rule is that the jury's determination of the facts may not be appealed, although an appeal of the trial judge's legal rulings is permitted.

■ PRISON

Prison is prison everywhere. Within each country there are, of course, differences from one facility to another: some are newer, some have more enlightened officials, some are less crowded than others. With only very few exceptions, though, there are not major differences in the average prison experience in the countries of Western Europe.

By and large, the prisons in Western Europe are comparable to the range of prisons in the United States: one would not likely find a Black Hole of Calcutta but, on the other hand, the facilities would probably be rated no better than from wretched to barely tolerable. They are places to stay out of if possible.

In any event, within broad latitude, the American will have to endure the same conditions as the nationals of the country where imprisoned. At some point, conditions may become so seriously deficient as to threaten substantially the health and safety of the prisoner and may constitute a violation of international human rights standards. In such circumstances, the American consulate should be available to complain to prison authorities on behalf of the American prisoner. As a practical matter, however, although the conditions of jails and prisons vary widely in Western Europe, it would be rare to find any so deficient as to violate human rights standards as currently interpreted.

Being a prisoner is always miserable. But being an American in a Western European prison can have its advantages and disadvantages, because of the intercession of the consular official and because—to be frank—Americans may receive preferential treatment in prison. (Keep in mind that Americans are not entitled to be treated any better than the country treats its own nationals. Prison officials may not discriminate against you for being an American, but they do not have to favor you either.) On the other hand, life for the American in prison abroad is harder than for nationals of that country, because the American is far from family and friends, unfamiliar with local procedures, practices and mores of the prison, and often not even able to speak the local language.

■ PRISONER RETURN TO THE UNITED STATES

In order to avoid the difficulties a country has maintaining foreign prisoners, as well as to alleviate the problems encountered by the foreign prisoner, many countries of Western Europe, and the United States, have signed the Council of Europe Convention on the Transfer of Sentenced Prisoners. As of the end of August 1985, the Convention was in effect between the United States, Spain, France, Sweden and the United Kingdom. It is expected that many other countries will also sign the Convention within the following few years.

The Convention is designed to provide a mechanism for transferring prisoners to their own country, where they may finish serving their sentences. Note that the transfer does not mean the prisoner will be set free, but only that the sentence may be served in an American prison rather than in a foreign prison.

The transfer of foreign prisoners is *not* automatic. A transfer may only take place if the following conditions are satisfied:

- The criminal proceedings in the foreign country must be over. Thus, a transfer may not happen before trial, if an appeal is not final or while any other aspect of the case is still pending.

- At the time of the transfer request, the prisoner must have at least 6 months left to serve.

- The crime committed by the prisoner must also be a crime in the prisoner's home country.

- The prisoner must consent to the transfer. Thus, a prisoner will not be involuntarily transfered back to his or her home country.

- The prisoner's home country must agree to take the prisoner in a transfer. Thus, the United States is not required to accept the transfer of all prisoners.

In the event an American is imprisoned in a Western European country that has signed this Convention, the United States consulate will provide information explaining the procedures for obtaining a transfer. Needless to say, the American should also discuss the matter with his or her lawyer.

Even this brief, general description of Western European criminal procedures should be sufficient to alert you to the complexity of the legal issues a criminal defendant must confront. Therefore, an American in trouble must find a capable and trustworthy lawyer, who is willing to answer your questions and calm your concerns. Fortunately that will be a lot easier to do in Western Europe than elsewhere in the world.

First, the consulate can be of help by providing a lawyers' list. In addition, although the consulate will not provide you with a recommendation, you should press the consulate official you talk to for as much information as possible about the experience and reputation of the lawyers on the list.

Second, as in the United States, word-of-mouth recommendations are probably the only way of assessing the skills of a lawyer in advance. Therefore, if you know anyone in the community, you should impose on those local contacts for the names of respected attorneys. Of course, unlike the lawyers on the consulate's list, all of whom speak English, a lawyer you learn about through a local contact may not speak your language, which is generally reason enough *not* to retain that person. (Your state of mind will depend to a large extent on establishing a close, working relationship with a lawyer with whom you can communicate freely, and that will be far less likely to happen if you need an interpreter to talk with your lawyer.)

Finally, you can contact friends or lawyers in this country who may know lawyers in the country where you are. Usually this will not be fast enough for your immediate needs right after arrest, and you will have to rely on a lawyer you can find quickly on the spot. However, if the proceedings are lengthy you will have a more time to make use of available resources in the United States.

III
COUNTRY-BY-COUNTRY ANALYSIS

1. AUSTRIA

U.S. Embassy and Consulates.

> Embassy and Consulate,
> Boltzmanngasse 16,
> Vienna, Tel. (222) 31-55-11;
> Consular Office,
> Giseladai 51,
> Salzburg, Tel. (662) 28-6-01

Passport and Visa Requirements for Incoming Americans. A U.S. citizen must have a valid passport to enter Austria. A visa is not required if the stay is for a period of three months or less. A tourist desiring to stay longer needs a visitor's visa, which can be obtained for a period of one year. When in the United States, inquiries and applications should be addressed to the Austrian consulates in this country (listed in Appendix C).

Residence. Americans desiring to reside in Austria permanently need an immigration visa, which can be approved only by the Federal Ministry of the Interior in Vienna, though application can be made at Austrian consulates in the United States.

Employment. In order for an American to be permitted to work in Austria, the prospective employer must first obtain a work permit for the American from the local Austrian employment office. That work permit must be presented by the individual to the consulate, which will then process the application for an employment visa.

The Austrian government warns that in order to obtain employment in Austria, "a thorough knowledge of German is essential, even for manual jobs. Clerical jobs require a perfect command of German, in speaking, writing and typing." Even with that language ability, Americans are discouraged from coming to Austria looking for work; jobs are generally not available, and when they are, they go first to Austrians.

Study. A student visa may be gotten for a one-year period upon application to an Austrian consulate. Applicant must present a letter of acceptance from an Austrian school or university.

Tourist Registration Requirements. Tourists must register with the Austrian authorities. If staying at a hotel, registration is automatic. Otherwise, travelers must register with the police (in major cities) or the Municipal Office (in rural areas).

A registration form (*Meldezettel*) may be purchased at any tobacco store and, after being completed and signed, delivered to the appropriate authorities. Any change of address must also be reported to the authorities. The traveler will be provided authenticated copies of the registration documentation. These are important travel documents in Austria and should be carefully retained. Failure to comply with the registration requirements can result in a fine of up to 3,000 Austrian schillings.

Customs Restrictions for Incoming Americans. American visitors to Austria may bring into the country, duty-free, all personal effects and possessions appropriate for wear and use while in Austria. These include wearing apparel, jewelry, toilet articles, two still and one movie cameras (each with ten rolls of film), a pair of binoculars, a musical instrument, a record player, a portable radio and TV, a tape recorder, a portable typewriter, sports equipmnt for personal use (including two sport rifles and 100 cartridges per rifle), and food for two days.

In order to be subject to the duty-free exemption, the foregoing articles must have been owned by the traveler, and in the traveler's possession, before departing for Austria. Furthermore, the articles must be intended for the traveler's personal use and not for sale in Austria.

In addition to the personal effects exemption, American travelers may import the following additional items duty-free (the numbers in parentheses are the amounts that may be imported from countries belonging to the EEC; however, for purposes of these customs regulations, any article purchased in a duty-free shop in any country is deemed to have been purchased outside the EEC):

- tobacco—400 (200) cigarettes or 100 (50) cigars or 500 (250) grams of tobacco; if mixed, proportionate amounts;

54

- liquor—1 (.75) liter;
- wine—2 (4) liters;
- perfume—one bottle, approx. 50 grams;
- cologne—one bottle, approx. 300 grams.

(The duty-free allowance for tobacco, liquor and wine is applicable only if the traveler is over 17 years of age.) In addition, any other items being carried as souvenirs (items intended for personal use or gifts, and not for commercial purposes) may be imported duty-free up to a total value of 1,000 Austrian schillings.

Currency Regulations and Banking. There are no restrictions on the amount of Austrian or foreign currency that may be brought into Austria.

A traveler may leave Austria with no limitation on the amount of foreign currency taken out of the country, but no more than Aus. 15,000 may be exported.

Note that foreign exchange transactions in Austria for purposes of capital investment; real estate purchases; purchases of stock in Austrian companies; and transfers of profits, dividends, interest, license fees and royalties can only be conducted if appropriate permits are issued by the Austrian National Bank. (For further information contact the Federal Ministry of Finance, Himmelpfortgasse 3, A-1010 Vienna, or the Austrian National Bank, Otto Wagner Platz 3, A-1090 Vienna.) The following are some of the American banks with branches located in Austria:

Citibank, Bank of America.
Lothringerstrasse 7
Postfach 90
Vienna
Tel. 75 65 34

The principal American Express offices are located at:

Kaerntnerstrasse 21/23
POB 288
Vienna
Tel. 52-05-44

Brixnerstrasse 3
Innsbruck, Tyrol
Tel. 22491, 27386

5 Mozartplatz
POB 244
Salzburg
Tel. 42501

Check with American Express for a complete list of its facilities throughout the country.

Health Requirements. No vaccinations are required of Americans, unless they have traveled through an area afflicted with disease.

Generally, Americans do not encounter any special health problems in Austria. In the event of medical emergency in Vienna, contact an ambulance by calling 144, or the Red Cross (*das Rote Kreuz*) at tel. 92-71-01. The General Hospital also handles emergencies: Allgemeines Krankemhaus der Stadt Wien, Alserstrasse 4, Vienna (tel. 4800).

Americans in need of medical assistance should contact the closest American consulate. The consulate will have a more complete list of hospital facilities, as well as a list of English-speaking doctors and health professionals. (See Section I:2.)

Automobile and Highway Regulations. Nonresident drivers must be at least 18 years old. Americans must have a driver's license from their state of residence as well as the international driver's license.

Driving in Austria is generally governed by rules of the road familiar to Americans.

Speed limits are typically 50 kilometers per hour (about 31 mph) in towns, 100 km/h (about 62 mph) on the open road, and 130 km/h (about 81 mph) on the highway.

Information about road conditions and traffic throughout the country is available, in English, every day of the week from 6 *A.M.* to 10 *P.M.* by calling the Austrian Automobile Club (*Osterreichischer Automobilklub*) at the following telephone number: (0222) 72997. The Automobile Club—located at Scubertring 3, Vienna (tel. 72-99)—is also a helpful source of information about automobile services, maps, routes, and driving requirements.

Art and Antiquities. There are no significant restrictions on the export of art or antiquities from Austria. If the item in question is under government protection—for example, the original artifacts of a castle subject to government regulation—government approval will be necessary.

Law and Criminal Justice. Austria is a parliamentary democracy. Because of its central location on the European continent, Austria has frequently been ravaged by war and torn between competing foreign powers. Indeed, it was not until as recently as 1955 that Austria was granted full sovereignty by the four allied powers (the United States, United Kingdom, France, and the USSR) that had partitioned the country after the World War II.

Interestingly, again because of that central location, Austria is now the most common country of asylum for refugees from the Communist-bloc countries of Eastern Europe.

Austria is a civil law country, and the Austrian criminal justice system functions in the continental tradition (as described in section II:8). Among its particular attributes are the following:

- After an arrest, a person may be held for a period of up to seventy-two hours for purposes of investigation. Thereafter, detention is permissible only if approved by the investigating judge.

- Bail is not uncommon in Austria, though it is not routine. Bail for foreign prisoners is usually quite substantial to offset the concern that the prisoner will leave the country. However, if the crime is subject to a sentence of ten years or more, then pretrial detention is mandatory and bail is not permitted.

- Most trials are conducted before one judge, or a panel of judges, sitting without a jury. However, Austria does provide for a trial by jury for the most serious offenses.

Austrian law does not make substantive distinctions among the various illegal drugs. Thus, for example, the penalties for trafficking in marijuana and cocaine are essentially the same.

---

2. BELGIUM

U.S. Embassy and Consulates.

Embassy and Consulate
27 Boulevard du Regent
Brussels
Tel. (02) 513-3830

Consular Office
Rubens Center
Nationalestraat 5
Antwerp
Tel. (03) 232-1800

Passport and Visa Requirements for Incoming Americans. U.S. citizens need a valid passport to enter Belgium. Tourists may stay in Belgium for three months without a visa. Subsequent three-month tourist stays are permissible only if separated by three months outside Belgium. In the United States, inquiries and applications should be addressed to the Belgian consulates in this country (listed in Appendix C).

Study. U.S. citizens need a student visa (*autorisation de sejour provisoire*) in order to travel to Belgium for purposes of study. The student visa, which must be obtained before leaving the United States, requires application at any Belgian consulate and the submission of appropriate documentation regarding means of support, certificate of enrollment from school, certificate of good health, and a police certificate.

Employment. Americans traveling to Belgium in order to work there, either employed or self-employed, must obtain a work visa (*autorisation de sejour provisoire*) before leaving the United States. According to the Belgian government, "No exceptions are made to this requirement." The visa can be obtained only after a work permit has been approved by officials in Belgium, therefore, the process may be time consuming.

Tourist Registration Requirements. Americans must register with the police within eight days of arriving in Belgium. If the traveler is staying in a hotel, registration is automatic. A traveler not staying in a hotel must register (*avis d'arrivee*) at the nearest city hall.

Customs Restrictions for Incoming Americans. Travelers may import, duty-free, all personal effects in their possession when entering Belgium.

In addition to the personal effects exemption, American travelers may import the following additional items duty-free (the numbers in parentheses are the amounts that may be imported from countries belonging to the EEC; however, for purposes of these customs regulations, any article purchased in a duty-free shop in any country is deemed to have been purchased outside the EEC):

- tobacco—400 (300) cigarettes or 200 (150) cigarillos or 100 (75) cigars or 500 (400) grams of smoking tobacco; if mixed, proportionate amounts;
- liquor—1 (1.5) liter if spirits contains more than 22 percent alcohol by volume, or 2 (3) liters if spirits contains less than 22 percent alcohol by volume, or 2 (3) liters of sparkling wine; if mixed, proportionately equivalent amounts;
- wine—2 (4) liters plus 8 liters of nonsparkling Luxembourg wine;
- perfume—50 (75) grams of perfume and 0.25 (0.375) liters of cologne; (The duty-free allowance for tobacco, liquor and wine is applicable only if the traveler is over 17 years of age.)

In addition, any other items being carried as souvenirs (items intended for personal use or gifts, and not for commercial purposes) may be imported duty-free up to a total value of

1,600 francs (except that only goods up to a value of 1,250 francs may come from non-EEC countries).

Currency Regulations and Banking. There are no currency regulations governing taking Belgian or foreign currency into, or out of, Belgium.

The following are some of the American banks with branches in Belgium:

> Citibank and Bank of America.
> Blvd. de Woluwe 2
> Brussels
> Tel. 762-0175

The principal American Express offices are located at:

> 2 Place Louise
> Brussels
> Tel. (02) 512-1740
>
> 87 Meir
> Antwerp
> Tel. (03) 232-5920

Check with American Express for a complete list of its facilities throughout the country.

Health and Hospitals. No vaccinations are required for entry into Belgium, but travelers from areas infected by cholera or yellow fever must prove proper vaccination as needed.

The Belgian nationwide emergency telephone number for calling an ambulance is 900. The Red Cross also provides an emergency ambulance service around the clock. In Brussels, it is located at Chaussee de Vleurgat, 80 (tel. 344-7010).

In an emergency, a doctor may be reached in Brussels at an official doctors' medical service, tel. 479-1818, or at the Centrale Telephonique Medicale, tel. 648-8000, which is a nonofficial service.

Americans in need of medical assistance should contact the closest American consulate. The consulate will have a more complete list of hospital facilities, as well as a list of English-speaking doctors and health professionals. (See Section I:2.)

Automobile and Highway Regulations. Americans may drive in Belgium with a valid passport and an American driver's license, or an international driver's license. Minimum driving age is 18.

Driving in Belgium is generally governed by rules of the road familiar to Americans. In addition, American drivers should observe the following rules:

- The "priority of the right" (*priorite de droite*, or *voorrang van rechts*), which one government publication describes as the "most important road rule"; although that may be a bit of an exaggeration, the fact is that Belgian drivers take that priority seriously. Thus, a Belgian driver approaching from the right, and having the right-of-way, will barrel through an intersection in circumstances where an American driver would normally at least slow down—and the American driver had best be alert;
- Seat belts must be worn;
- The car must be equipped with an International Warning Triangle, which must be displayed in an emergency breakdown.

Speed limits are typically 60 kilometers per hour (about 37 mph) in towns; 90 km/h (about 56 mph) on the open road; and 120 km/h (about 74 mph) on the highway.

In the event of an emergency, the Royal Automobile Club de Belgique operates an SOS number: tel. (02) 736-5959. In addition, roadside telephones are connected to the general "emergency coordinator" at tel. 9. Belgium also has a fleet of little yellow cars, called Touring Secours or just TS, that stop to assist drivers in trouble. The Touring Secours can be easily summoned by pulling off to the side of the road and raising the hood of the car.

Be aware also that there are two automobile clubs that can be contacted for information and travel assistance:

Royal Automobile Club de Belgique
Rue d'Arlon, 53
1040 Brussels
Tel. (02) 513-3855 or 512-9200)

Touring Club de Belgique
Rue de la Loi, 44
1040 Brussels
Tel. (02) 513-8240 or 512-7890

Art and Antiquities. There are no restrictions on exporting art from Belgium.

Law and Criminal Justice. Belgium is a parliamentary democracy under the rule of a monarch. Although the country has a stable political history, it has recently suffered a rash of terrorist attacks, mostly on multinational corporations in Brussels. As a result, the Brussels police are very much in view and are often carrying heavy-duty weaponry.

The police have the power to stop people on the street, without cause, and ask for the identification papers issued to all

Belgians. That documentation must be carried at all times. Americans would, therefore, be advised to carry their passports with them when out and about.

Belgium is a civil law country, and the Belgian criminal justice system functions in the Continental tradition (as described in Section II:8). Among its particular attributes are the following:

- Police may interrogate a prisoner for an initial period of twenty-four hours. They then must bring the prisoner before the Judge of Instruction, who will decide whether the prisoner may be held for as much as another four days. During that period, the prisoner does not have a right to see a lawyer.

- The general rule is that pretrial confinement is not preferred, except in certain special circumstances, among which are the risk that the prisoner will flee the jurisdiction, which of course generally applies to virtually all non-Belgians, and certain serious offenses, such as drug offenses.

- Bail technically exists, but is rarely used and even less so for a foreigner, because a foreigner does not have the ties to the community that would ensure his return.

During the course of the normal instruction of the case (the investigation), the defense counsel would not be present, usually not even when the defendant gives a statement.

The drug laws in Belgium do not distinguish dramatically among different drugs, or different acts (that is, possession or trafficking, for example). However, in practice, the Belgian authorities do not appear to be focussing on the small personal-use offenses. On the other hand, there are a sizable number of trafficking cases which the authorities prosecute vigorously. Typically, these cases involve quantities of a kilo or more of drugs, which, upon conviction, will result in a sentence of about three to five years, depending on the circumstance, and perhaps even more if the prisoner has been knowingly working for an organized crime operation.

---

3. F R A N C E

U.S. Embassy and Consulates.

Embassy and Consulate
2 Avenue Gabriel
Paris
Tel. 296-1202

Consular Office
No. 9 Rue Armeny
Marseille
Tel. 54-92-00

Consular Office
22 Cours du Marechal Foch
Bordeaux
Tel. 52-65-95

Consular Office
1 Rue du Marechal Joffre
Nice
Tel. (93) 88-89-55 and 88-87-72

Consular Office
7 Quai General Sarrall
Lyon
Tel. 824-68-49

Consular Office
15 Avenue d'Alsace
Strasbourg
Tel. (88) 35-31-04 through -06

Passport and Visa Requirements for Incoming Americans. An American must have a valid passport to enter France and can then travel in France for up to ninety days without a visa.

Residence. A person desiring to stay in France for an extended period of time must obtain a long stay visa. The application form (which, the government specifically emphasizes, must be completed in French) maybe obtained from a French consulate in the United States (listed in Appendix C). It requires the applicant to provide (i) detailed information about the purpose of the trip; (ii) information regarding the applicant's means of support while in France; (iii) the name of at least one reference in France, or a letter of invitation from a company or mission concerning the applicant's trip to France; and (iv) six passport-size photographs. The application is then submitted to the consulate, which must send it to officials in France for approval. The government advises that a delay of two-three months is possible, so the traveler should plan accordingly.

Employment. An American desiring to work in France must first obtain a job offer from a French employer. The employer then files an application for working papers on behalf of the prospective employee at the Office National d'Immigration. If the papers are approved, the file is sent to the consulate closest to the individual's residence in this country. The government warns, "Under no circumstances are working papers issued to the applicant in France, even if the foreign worker is temporarily in France when the authorization is granted."

For the last decade, the employment of foreign nationals in

France (other than the nationals of European Common Market countries) has been subject to a virtual freeze because of high domestic unemployment. According to the American consulate, these laws "governing immigration and employment in France are being enforced with increasing rigor." Therefore, it is extremely difficult, if not impossible, for an American to obtain employment in France.

Study. Americans desiring to study in France must also obtain a visa. Inasmuch as the student visa is issued by the consulate, rather than officials in France, it can be obtained in only twenty-four hours. Therefore, students are advised not to apply for visas too far in advance of departure. The American student may obtain an application, which can be completed in French or English, at any French consulate.

In addition, the applicant must have (i) a valid passport (the expiration date of the passport must exceed the expiration date of the visa by at least two months); (ii) a letter of admission from the school; (iii) notarized statements of financial guarantee assuring a monthly allowance of at least $450; (iv) if the student is under 18 years of age, the parents must submit a letter stating the name of an individual in France appointed as guardian during the student's stay there; (v) a certificate of good health from a physician; (vi) two passport-size photographs.

Tourist Registration Requirements. There are no tourist registration requirements in France.

Customs Restrictions for Incoming Americans. American visitors to France may bring into the country, duty-free, all personal articles currently in use including: clothes, jewelry (maximum weight 500 grams, or approx. 1 lb.), toilet articles baby carriage, one movie and two still cameras (each with ten rolls of film), a pair of binoculars, a musical instrument, a record player, a portable radio and TV, a portable video tape recorder and video camera, a tape recorder, a portable typewriter, sports equipment for personal use (including two sport rifles and 100 cartridges per rifle), and a pocket calculator.

In addition to the personal effects exemption, American travelers may import the following additional items duty-free (the numbers in parentheses are the amounts that may be imported from countries belonging to the EEC; however, for purposes of these customs regulations, any article purchased in a duty-free shop in any country is deemed to have been purchased outside the EEC):

- tobacco—400 (200) cigarettes or 200 (150) cigarillos or 100 (50) cigars or 500 (250) grams of tobacco;

- liquor—1 (1.5) liter if more than 22 percent alcohol content and 2 (3) liters if 22 percent alcohol content or less;
- wine—2 (4) liters;
- perfume—50 (75) grams;
- cologne—200 (300) grams.

(The duty-free allowance for tobacco, liquor and wine is applicable only if the traveler is over 17 years of age.)

In addition, any other items brought into the country may be imported duty free up to a total value of $300 (1,400 French francs).

The importation of raw gold (bars, ingots, etc.) is forbidden except in cases where prior approval has been obtained from the Bank of France.

Currency Regulations and Banking. There are no restrictions on bringing any currency into France. However, a traveler with foreign currency in excess of 5,000 Fr. in value, who intends to leave France again with that amount, must obtain a declaration form which, when certified, will permit the removal of the currency when the French stay is completed.

The traveler may leave France with no more than 5,000 Fr. And the traveler may not leave France with any foreign currency in excess of 5,000 Fr. value unless the currency was declared upon arrival.

The following are some of the American banks with branches in France:

Citibank, N.A.;
26 Avenue des Champs Elysees
Paris
Tel. 562 7676

Bank of America;
43/47 Avenue de l;a Grande Armee
Paris
Tel. 501 5412

Chemical Bank
190 Avenue Charles de Gaulle
Paris
Tel. 637 6565

The principal American Express offices are located at:

11 Rue Scribe
Paris
Tel 266-0999

8 Rue Chidebert
Cannes
Tel. 381-587

6 Rue Childert
Lyon
Tel. 837-4069

Check with American Express for a complete list of its facilities throughout the country.

Health and Hospitals. There are no vaccination requirements for Americans entering France.

Tourists do not generally encounter any special health problems in France.

Americans in need of medical assistance should contact the closest American consulate. The consulate will have a more complete list of hospital facilities, as well as a list of English-speaking doctors and health professionals. (See Section I:2.)

Automobile and Highway Regulations. Americans are authorized to drive in France if they have either an international driver's license or a valid American license. (French regulations are currently under review and an American license may not be sufficient in the future. The safest option is to obtain the international license.) Driving in France is generally governed by rules of the road familiar to Americans. Americans should be aware of the following special requirements:

- drivers must be 18 years old, even if entitled to drive at a younger age in the United States;
- seat belts are mandatory;
- spare bulbs for headlights must be carried;
- the car must be equipped with warning lights or a phosphorescent warning triangle to be used in case of a breakdown;
- horns may be used only when absolutely necessary and are prohibited in Paris (and certain other towns) except in case of immediate danger;
- yellow headlights are compulsory on French cars, and it is highly recommended that foreign cars obtain yellow disc adaptors to convert white lights;
- drivers on major roads have a priority over entering traffic; in all other cases, when two cars approach an intersection, the car on the right has priority;
- pedestrians using pedestrian crossings, or getting on or off a bus or trolley, have the right-of-way;

Speed limits are typically 60 kilometers per hour (about 37

mph) in towns, 90 km/h (about 56 mph) on the open road, and 130 km/h (about 81 mph) on the highway.

The French Automobile Club (Touring Club de France) has established an emergency patrol network to assist drivers in trouble. It is called *Touring Secours*. To obtain Touring Secours assistance, contact the Touring Club de France, 6-8 Rue Firmin-Gillot, 75737 Paris Cedex 15 (tel. 532-2215).

In the event of an accident, the driver should immediately inform the Bureau Central Francais des Societes Assurances contre les Accidents d'Automobiles, 118 Rue de Tocqueville, 75017 Paris (tel. 766-5264).

Art and Antiquities. In order to export any art or antiquities deemed by France to be "national treasures," the purchaser will need the approval of two government agencies:

> SAFICO
> (Service des Autorisations
>   Financiales et Commerciales)
> 42 Rue de Clichy
> Paris
> Tel. 281-9144
>
> Directions Generales Des Douanes et
>   Droits Indirects
> 8 Rue de la Tours des Dames
> Paris
> Tel. 280-6722

In most instances, such art will be purchased from a gallery or dealer, and the seller will normally take care of all the red tape. As described by one government official, obtaining the necessary approval "is a slow, bureaucratic process," and it would be difficult for the American to complete the formalities personally (unless, of course, fluent in French and familiar with the peculiarities of the French bureaucracy).

These restrictions will not apply to most purchases made by the Americans. If you are concerned, the seller should provide you with the necessary information, or you can contact SAFICO directly.

Law and Criminal Justice. France is a parliamentary republic under the leadership of a president. The current Fifth French Republic was established by Gen. Charles de Gaulle in 1958, and since that time the basic structure of the French government has remained stable. However, during the life of the Fifth Republic the country has experienced considerable political turmoil, from the Algerian self-determination uprisings of the early 1960s to the current rise in political terrorism.

Although most of the recent terrorist acts seem to involve

Arab politics, in March 1984 an unsuccessful attack was made on the life of the U.S. consul in Strasbourg, France, and the U.S. government has stated, "The threat level against U.S. officials in France remains very high and attacks against private U.S. citizens cannot be ruled out."

France is a civil law country, and the French criminal justice system functions in the Continental tradition (as described in Section II:8). Among its particular attributes are the following:

- After an arrest, a suspect can be held and interrogated by the police for as long as two days before being brought before a judge. In drug cases, that period may be extended by two days, for a total of four days of interrogation. The prisoner is generally not permitted to see a lawyer during this interrogation period, although thereafter the defense lawyer may be present during all questioning of the defendant by the judge of instruction.

- The total period of pretrial confinement permitted is normally four months for misdemeanors (although that period may be extended an additional four months in exceptional circumstances). However, there are no legal limits on the length of pretrial confinement in felony cases.

- The judge of instruction who conducts the investigation of the case will also decide on whether the defendant should remain in pretrial confinement. Generally, in serious cases, the practice in France is that defendants are not released from custody before trial, particularly in drug cases. That practice applies with even greater effect to assure the appearance at trial of foreigners having no ties to the community. Bail is technically available, though it is rarely granted.

- France does permit jury trials, but only in the *cours d'assises* (assize courts), which hear the serious felony cases. The less serious cases are tried in the *tribunaux correctionnels* (correctional courts) without jury.

- The provisions of Continental law that often permit a victim to participate in the criminal proceedings (see Section II:8) are applied in France to allow the French customs authorities to participate in smuggling cases (including drug smuggling). If the defendant is found guilty, an additional "customs" fine may be imposed, which may also result in additional detention if that fine is not paid.

Recent revisions of the drug laws in France distinguish between use and dealing. The use of illegal drugs, though still illegal, is considered an illness and is handled as a a health problem rather than as a criminal problem. According to the French government, drug use is treated like "other social problems such as alcoholism and venereal disease." On the other hand,

the new laws increase the penalties for the production and trafficking in drugs up to a maximum possible sentence per offense of 20 years and a 50-million-franc fine (formerly, the
maximum possible imprisonment was only 5 years).

Generally, personal-use offenses are not a high investigative
priority of the French authorities, though if a case comes to police attention—for example, if drugs are discovered in the possession of an individual while crossing the border—the case
may be pursued vigorously. Possession itself, particularly of
more than small amounts, may be deemed evidence of dealing
and handled accordingly.

---

4. G E R M A N Y
(The Federal Republic of Germany)

U.S. Embassy and Consulates.

> Embassy and Consulate
> Delchmannsaue, 5300
> Bonn
> Tel. (0228) 339-3390

> Consular Office
> Alsterufer 27/28
> Hamburg
> Tel. (040) 44-10-61

> Consular Office
> Clayallee 170
> Berlin
> Tel. (030) 819-7561

> Consular Office
> Koeniginstrasse 5
> Muenchen
> Tel. (089) 2-30-11

> Consular Office
> Cecillenallee 5
> Duesseldorf
> Tel. (0211) 49-00-81

> Consular Office
> Urbanstrasse 7
> Stuttgart
> Tel. (0711) 21-02-21

> Consular Office
> Siesmayerstrasse 21
> Frankfurt
> Tel. (0611) 74-00-71

Passport and Visa Requirements for Incoming Americans. U.S. citizens need a valid passport to enter Germany. A visa is not required for a stay of up to three months, as long as the traveler does not obtain employment in Germany.

American travelers who are not citizens of the United States (i.e., U.S. resident aliens) who are traveling outside the United States on a "Permit to Reenter" must have a visa to enter Germany irrespective of the duration of the stay. A visa can be obtained from German consulates upon presentation of a round-trip ticket back to the United States.

Residence. Americans desiring to remain in Germany for an extended stay (that is, longer than the three-month tourist period), for any purpose, must obtain a residence permit. It can be obtained in Germany from the local police authorities upon presentation of the following documentation:

- a good-conduct certificate, which is the individual's own statement that the American has no misdemeanor or felony convictions and is at least 16 years old;

- a medical certificate (*Gesundheitszeugnis fuer Aufenhaltserlaubnis*) completed by a German doctor attesting to good health.

When in the United States, inquiries and applications should be addressed to the German consulates in this country (listed in Appendix C).

Employment. An American intending to work in Germany must have a visa. The German government recommends that application for a visa be made while the traveler is still in the United States, rather than after arriving in Germany as a tourist, because the processing may not be completed before the three-month tourist period expires and the traveler will suffer "inconveniences in case the application is denied" or delayed. According to the government, "A residence permit (visa) can only be given with the approval of the appropriate local office for aliens in Germany. This procedure might take eight to twelve weeks, sometimes even more."

Beware, however, of the employment situation in Germany. More so than most other countries, the large U.S. Army presence in Germany means that the country is fairly well saturated with young Americans, recently discharged from the service, who are looking for jobs permitting them to stay in the country. As a result of generally high unemployment and the abundance of ex-servicemen, the American consulate states: "It is almost impossible for American citizens to find employment in Germany, and even those employed can seldom maintain the standard of living to which they are accustomed, on the salaries offered."

DISCARD GRACE COLLEGE LIBRARY
Winona Lake, Indiana

69

Tourist Registration Requirements. Americans staying in Germany, in a hotel, for longer than eight weeks must register with the local police, even though they may stay in the country for 12 weeks without a visa. Americans staying in private homes in Germany must register with the police if they remain in the country for more than one week.

Customs Restrictions for Incoming Americans. A traveler's personal effects and equipment may be brought into Germany without duty or customs declaration.

Americans may also import the following items into Germany duty-free (numbers in parentheses refer to amounts that may be imported from countries belonging to the EEC; however, for purposes of these customs regulations, any article purchased in a duty-free shop in any country is deemed to have been purchased outside the EEC):

- tobacco—400 cigarettes or 200 cigarillos or 100 cigars; if in mixed amounts, a total of 500 grams;
- liquor—1 (1.5) liter if more than 22 percent alcohol by volume, or 2 (3) liters if less than 22 percent alcohol by volume, or 2 (3) liters of sparkling wine; if mixed, proportionately equivalent amounts;
- wine—2 (4) liters;
- perfume—50 (75) grams of perfume and 0.25 (0.375) liters of cologne;
- coffee—250 (750) grams of coffee or 100 (300) grams of instant coffee;
- tea—100 (150) grams of tea. (The duty-free allowance of tobacco, liquor and wine is applicable only if the traveler is over 17 years of age, and 15 years of age for coffee.)

In addition, any other items being carried as souvenirs (items intended for personal use or gifts, and not for commercial purposes) may be imported duty-free up to a total value of DM 460, provided, however, that only DM 115 of that total may be goods from non-EEC countries. The "souvenir" exemption does not apply to unworked gold, gold alloys, or rolled gold.

All duty-free allowances are applicable only if the particular imported goods are in the personal possession of the traveler at the time of entering Germany.

Currency Regulations and Banking. There are no restrictions on the import and export of German DM or any other currency.

Foreign currency or traveler's checks can be exchanged at all banks, and exchange offices can be found at travel centers such as airports and train stations.

The following are some of the American banks with branches in Germany:

Bank of America,
Mainzer Landstrasse 46
P.O. Box 110243
Frankfurt (Main)
Tel. 75621

Visa Card Services
Eschersheimer Landstrasse 14
P.O. Box 4549
Frankfurt
Tel. 15460

Ludwigstrasse 8-10
P.O. Box 423
Munich 22
Tel. 21330

Citibank Aktiengesellschaft,
Grosse Gallusstrasse 16
Postfach 110333
Frankfurt
Tel. 13660

Ernst-Teuter-Platz 305
Postfach 126070
Berlin
Tel. 3137084

Odeonsplatz 12
Postfach 447
Munich
Tel. 237200

Chemical Bank.
Ulmenstrasse 30
P.O. Box 174126
Frankfurt
Tel. 71581

The principal American Express offices are located at:

Kurfuerstendamm
Berlin
Tel. 882-7575

Promenadplatz 6
Munich
Tel. 21990

Steinweg 5
Frankfurt
Tel. 21051

Check with American Express for a complete list of its facilities throughout the country.

Health and Hospitals. Americans traveling in Germany do not face any special health risks. Americans in need of medical assistance should contact the closest American consulate. The consulate will have a more complete list of hospital facilities, as well as a list of English-speaking doctors and health professionals. (See Section I:2 on U.S. consular services.)

Automobile and Highway Regulations. Americans may drive in Germany for one year with:

- an international driver's license; or
- an American driver's license, if accompanied by a German translation.

Driving in Germany is generally governed by rules of the road familiar to Americans. However, American travelers should be aware of the following special rules:

- the use of seat belts is mandatory;
- children are not allowed to sit in the front seat; passing on the right is strictly forbidden.

One of the most distinctive aspects of driving in Germany is that there is no speed limit on the highway (Autobahn), although the recommended maximum speed is 130 km/h (about 81 mph). Otherwise, speed limits are typically 50 kilometers per hour (about 31 mph) in towns and 100 km/h (about 62 mph) on the open road.

Germany has three automobile clubs, all of which provide information and aid to the traveler throughout the country:

Algemeiner Deutscher Automobil Club (ADAC)
Baumgartnerstrasse 53
D-8000 Munchen 70
Tel. (089) 76761

Automobilclub von Deutschland (AvD)
Lyonerstrasse 16
D-6000 Frankfurt/Mein
Tel. (0611) 66061

Deutscher Touring Automobil Club (DTC)
Amalienburgstrasse 23
D-8000 Munchen 60
Tel. (089) 8111048/9

Each of the clubs maintains a breakdown service which can be contracted through telephone information in most cities in Germany.

Art and Antiquities. There are no restrictions on the export of art or antiquities from Germany.

Law and Criminal Justice. Germany is a federal republic with a democratic parliamentary government. The state governments (Lander) have considerable autonomy in matters pertaining to criminal justice (thus, procedural generalizations are difficult). However, it is fair to say generally that since the war—in part because of the American influence in shaping the country's legal system—the rights of criminal suspects are protected better than in most, if not all, other countries of continental Western Europe.

Germany is a civil law country, and the German criminal justice system functions in the Continental tradition (as described in Section II:8). Its particular attributes are as follows:

- The police must bring any arrested prisoner before a judge no later than the end of the day following the arrest. The judge will then determine whether further pretrial detention is warranted.

- A bail procedure exists, but it is rarely used and even less likely to be granted to a foreigner because of a fear that the defendant will flee. Furthermore, bail will not likely be permitted in drug cases.

- German law does not provide for jurors in the American sense. However, many of the more serious crimes are tried in courts that consist of both professional judges and lay judges (that is, people from the community who sit with the judges to determine the case).

Drugs are a problem in Germany, particularly for the large population of young American men in Germany who have stayed in the country after discharge from the army. In the last few years the Germans have increased the penalties for drug offenses and the Germans have a reputation of dealing severely with drugs, particularly trafficking. There are many Americans in German jails for drug offenses. Therefore, the American would be well advised not to travel with drugs into Germany, particularly when coming from the Netherlands or other countries known for their drug trade.

---

5. GREECE

U.S. Embassy and Consulates.

Embassy and Consulate
92 Vasllissis Sophias Boulevard
Athens
Tel. 721-2951

Consular Office
59 Leoforos Nikis
Thessaloniki
Tel. 266-121

Passport and Visa Requirements for Incoming Americans. American citizens are required to have a valid passport to enter Greece. They may stay for a period of three months without a visa. A traveler desiring to stay longer may obtain a permit from the Aliens Bureau, 9 Halkokondili Street, Athens (tel. 3628.301). In the United States, inquiries and applications should be addressed to the Greek consulates in this country (listed in Appendix C).

The permit, which will be issued only upon proving that the traveler has means of support, is valid for a total stay in Greece of six months from the time of original entry. For the most part, the Greek authorities will continue to renew the permit every six months, as long as the American can demonstrate that he or she is self-supporting on funds imported from abroad, or is in possession of a valid work permit.

Employment. Americans desiring to work (or study) in Greece must be in possession of valid visas and residence permits. These documents should be applied for and obtained before arriving in Greece.

A notice put out by the American consulate in Athens succinctly tells the whole story about the likelihood of Americans finding employment in Greece: "Opportunities for employment in Greece for non-Greek citizens are extremely limited....It is to be noted that because of high unemployment in Greece, work permits are rarely granted to aliens." In fact, even employment with American firms cannot be expected because all foreign business is strictly limited in the number of non-Greek employees it may hire.

Tourist Registration Requirements. There are no tourist registration requirements in Greece.

Customs Restrictions for Incoming Americans. A traveler's personal effects and equipment may be brought into Greece without duty or customs formalities.

Americans may also import the following items into Greece duty-free (the numbers in parentheses refer to amounts that may be imported from countries belonging to the EEC; however, for purposes of these customs regulations, any article purchased in a duty-free shop in any country is deemed to have been purchased outside the EEC):

- tobacco—200 (300) cigarettes or 100 (150) cigarillos or 50 (75) cigars or 250 (400) grams of tobacco;
- liquor—1 (1.5) liter if more than 22 percent alcohol by volume, or 2 (3) liters if less than 22 percent alcohol by volume, or 2 (3) liters of sparkling wine;
- wine—2 (4) liters;
- perfume—50 (75) grams of perfume and 0.25 (0.375) liters of cologne;
- coffee—500 (750) grams of coffee or 200 (300) grams of instant coffee;
- tea—100 (150) grams of tea. (The duty-free allowance for tobacco, liquor and wine is applicable only if the traveller is over 17 years of age, and 15 years of age for coffee.)

In addition, any other items that are not of a commercial nature may be imported duty-free up to a total value of 2,850 (11,000) drs., provided, however, that if the traveler is under the age of 15, the duty-free exemption is only 1,450 (3,100) drs.

Currency Regulations and Banking. Foreign currency, notes, and gold may be imported into Greece without limitation. However, only 1,500 drs. may be imported into the country.

Americans may leave Greece with no more than $500 (or equivalent foreign currency amounts) unless the traveler declared the amount of currency being brought into Greece at the entry checkpoint. The government warns, "Declarations of foreign currency imported are acceptable only at the moment of entry of the foreign visitor to Greece."

Traveler's checks and bank checks in the name of the traveler and drawn in foreign currency may be taken out of Greece without restriction.

It is forbidden (without Bank of Greece approval) to send out of Greece by any means, including the mail, currency, banknotes, traveler's checks, payment orders "or any other values" whether in Greek or foreign currency.

The Greek authorities are very strict about currency control regulations. A traveler having questions about these regulations should contact the Directorate for the Protection of National Currency, Ministry of Public Order, 10 Stadiou Street, Athens (tel. 3221-716).

The following are some of the American banks with branches in Athens:

Citibank, N.A.;
8, Othonos Str.
P.O. Box 11017
Athens 10310
Tel. 3227-471

Bank of America.
39 Panepistimiou St.,
Athens
Tel. 325 1909 thru 19

The principal American Express offices are located at:

Constitution Square
Box 3325
2 Hermou Street
Tel. 3244-975

Venizelou Street, 10
Salonica
Tel. (031) 225-302

Check with American Express for a complete list of its facilities throughout the country.

Health and Hospitals. Vaccination certificates are not usually required for Greece; however, entry to Greece from certain areas in the Mideast and Africa may require vaccination depending on disease conditions.

There are no special health problems in Greece. The water is usually safe to drink throughout the country.

In the event of medical emergency there are a number of hospitals in Athens:

Alexandras
Vas. Sophias Avenue and Lourou Street
Athens
Tel. 777-0501 through 04

Erythros Stavros
Erythrou Stavrou and Lourou Streets
Athens
Tel. 691-0512 and -7030

Apostolos Pavlos "Kat"
(Accidents' Hospital)
2, Nikis Street
Kifissia
Tel. 801-4730 through 39

Americans in need of medical assistance should contact the closest American consulate. The consulate will have a more complete list of hospital facilities, as well as a list of English-speaking doctors and health professionals. (See Section I:2 on U.S. consular services.)

Automobile and Highway Regulations. Americans are permitted to drive in Greece only with an international driver's li-

cense. In Greece the international driver's license can be obtained from a Greek automobile touring Club (ELPA) office
upon presentation of an American driver's license, a passport,
a photograph and drs. 6 Driving in Greece is generally governed by rules of the road familiar to Americans. The International Warning Triangle must be carried and used in the event
of a breakdown.

Speed limits are typically 50 kilometers per hour (about 31
mph) in towns, and 100 km/h (about 62 mph) on the open
roads and highways.

Automobile information and assistance may be obtained
from any Greek Automobile Touring Club (ELPA) located
throughout the country. The main office is at:

> 2-4 Messogion Street,
> Athens,
> Tel. (01) 7791-6

In the event of an automobile breakdown, ELPA road assistance service can be reached by dialing 104 anywhere in the
country. The road assistance service is available 24 hours a
day in Athens and Thessaloniki, and from 7 *A.M.* to 10 *P.M.* in
most other places in the country.

Art and Antiquities. Greek antiquities have been pillaged by
travelers from the rest of the world for hundreds of years, and
the Greeks will not allow that to happen any longer. The Greek
authorities have very strict rules prohibiting the removal of art
or antiquities from Greece.

In order to remove antiquities from Greece the traveler must
obtain the permission of the Archeological Section of the Ministry of Culture and Sciences, located at 13 Polignotou Street,
Athens (tel. 321-9860).

If the item in question is purchased from a shop, the receipt
must state that the item must be taken to appropriate Greek
authorities for approval. Usually, the shop will take care of all
the formalities, and certainly the traveler should insist that it do
so. If the item is purchased from some source other than a
shop, the item may be personally taken to the Archeological
Section. These clearance procedures may take as much as a
month to complete, and if the traveler should no longer be in
Greece by that time, arrangements for shipment will also have
to be made.

Anyone caught leaving Greece with an antiquity that has not
been cleared by the authorities will definitely have the item
confiscated, and may be fined or held for some other criminal
penalty. This is considered a very serious offense in Greece.

Check with American Express for a complete list of its facilities throughout the country.

Law and Criminal Justice. Greece today is a presidential republic, with a parliament democratically elected by the people. In the last 20 years, Greece has suffered a great deal of political turmoil that has seen the end of the monarchy, as well as more than one military coup. One current manifestation of that agitated political history is the increase in political, and public, murders and other acts of seemingly random terrorism. For example, in 1984 alone seven murders, including the assassination of the British cultural affairs officer, were attributed to Arab terrorists. So far there have not been reports of tourists being either the subject of, or inadvertently caught up in, the violence.

Greece is a civil law country, and the Greek criminal justice system functions in the Continental tradition (as described in Section II:8). Among its particular attributes are the following:

- Upon his or her arrest for a serious offense, including drug offenses, the police may hold a prisoner incommunicado and interrogate the prisoner for three days, which may be extended if needed. During this initial investigatory period, the prisoner is not entitled to a lawyer. However, there is a right to counsel before a person is required to sign any statement, such as a confession.

- Bail is permitted in Greece. Application is made, first, to the district attorney (the *eisanghelefs*), who may approve it with or without conditions (such as periodic reporting to the police authorities). If the district attorney disapproves the bail application, the prisoner may appeal that decision to the court.

- Mail to and from prisoners in Greece is censored, which not only intrudes on the privacy of that correspondence but also greatly delays it because of the difficulties of translation.

The Greek government is very serious about enforcing its currency control regulations. Many Americans, particularly those of Greek origin, have gotten in trouble in the past by trying to circumvent those restrictions. Typically, the American is trying to bring money into the country to help family or friends, or trying to remove money from the country for foreign investment. In either case, the Greek authorities scrutinize people of Greek background carefully.

Greece also has strict drug laws. Like many countries of Western Europe, Greek law makes no distinction among different types of illegal drugs. Thus the statutory penalties for possession, for example, are the same regardless of the drug. Of course, in practice, the courts tend to treat the "hard" drugs more severely.

Keep in mind that the drug laws, as written, are relatively severe, and the discretionary decision to be more lenient than necessary can be changed at any time. Moreover, even if the authorities are being somewhat less aggressive in punishing the personal-use possession cases, they have not noticeably diminished the intensity of their efforts against drug trafficking through Greece.

6.   I R E L A N D

U.S. Embassy and Consulate.

Embassy and Consulate
42 Elgin Road
Ballsbridge, Dublin
Tel. 688777

Passport and Visa Requirements for Incoming Americans. American citizens must have a valid passport to enter Ireland. For a stay of three months or less, no visa is required. Tourists intending to stay in Ireland longer than three months must register at the nearest police station. When in the United States, inquiries and applications should be addressed to the Irish consulates in this country (listed in Appendix C).

Employment. An American desiring to work in Ireland must first be granted a work permit and visa. The work permit must be obtained by the employer, upon application to the Ministry for Labor, Mespil Road, Dublin. Work permits for foreigners will be granted only for highly specialized and skilled work for which there are no available Irish applicants. After the work permit is granted, the individual may make application for a visa at any Irish consulate in this country.

Because of severe unemployment in Ireland, it is extremely difficult for an American to obtain a job in Ireland. Therefore, the American consulate warns, "Americans are urged not to come to Ireland with the expectation of finding employment unless they have an assured source of income before their arrival, or some definite understanding with their prospective employers, who have already obtained work permits on their behalf."

Tourist Registration Requirements. There are no tourist registration requirements in Ireland.

Customs Restrictions for Incoming Americans. Travelers may import, duty-free, all personal effects in their possession when entering Ireland, on the understanding that all such personal effects will be taken with the traveler again when leaving Ireland. (In the case of especially valuable items admitted into Ireland under the "personal effects" exemption, the traveler may be required to leave a deposit on the duty which would otherwise be charged, but the deposit will be refunded at the time of departure from Ireland upon production of the items in question and the deposit receipt.) In addition to the personal effects exemption, American travelers may import the following additional items duty-free (the numbers in parentheses are the amounts that may be imported from countries belonging to the EEC; however, for purposes of these customs regulations, any article purchased in a duty-free shop in any country is deemed to have been purchased outside the EEC):

- tobacco—400 (300) cigarettes or 200 (150) cigarillos or 100 (75) cigars or 500 (400) grams of smoking tobacco;
- liquor—1 (1.5) liter if spirits contain more than 22 percent alcohol by volume, or 2 (3) liters if spirits contain less than 22 percent alcohol by volume, or 2 (3) liters of sparkling wine;
- wine—2 (4) liters;
- perfume—50 (75) grams of perfume and 0.25 (0.375) liters of cologne. (The duty-free allowance for tobacco, liquor or wine is applicable only if traveler is over 17 years of age.)

In addition, any other items being carried for personal use or gifts, and not for commercial purposes, may be imported duty-free up to a total value of L27 (L120, except that no one item may exceed L52).

All duty-free allowances are applicable only if the particular imported goods are in the personal possession of the traveler at the time of entering Ireland.

Currency Regulations and Banking. There are no restrictions on the import of Irish or foreign currency.

Americans leaving Ireland can take out no more than L100 in Irish currency. However, there are no restrictions on exporting any amount of traveler's or bank checks issued in Irish pounds. And there are no restrictions on taking out foreign currency or checks in any amount.

The following are some of the American banks with branches in Ireland:

Bank of America;
26-27 Grafton Street
Dublin
Tel. 775 404

Citibank, N.A.
71 St. Stephens's Green
Dublin
Tel. 780 488

The principal American Express office is located at:

116 Grafton Street
Dublin
Tel. 772874

Check with American Express for a complete list of its facilities throughout the country.

Health and Hospitals. There are no vaccination requirements for entry into Ireland, except that an international certificate of vaccination against smallpox will be required if the traveler has been, within the preceding 14 days, to a country any part of which is infected.

Travelers in Ireland do not generally encounter any special health problems.

Americans in need of medical assistance should contact the closest American consulate. The consulate will have a more complete list of hospital facilities, as well as a list of English-speaking doctors and health professionals. (See Section I:2 on U.S. consular services.)

Automobile and Highway Regulations. Americans may drive in Ireland with an international driver's license.

Beware: The Irish, like the British, drive on the left side of the road. Aside from that adjustment, driving in Ireland is generally governed by rules of the road familiar to Americans. However, be sure to observe the following special rules:

• drivers and front-seat passengers must wear seat belts;
• children under 12 may not ride in the front seat.

The national speed limit is 55 mph (88 km/h) on the open roads. The limit in towns is typically between 30 and 40 mph (48 and 64 km/h).

Driver's assistance and information may be obtained from the Automobile Association, 23 Suffolk Street, Dublin.

Art and Antiquities. There are no restrictions on the export of art and antiquities from Ireland. However, archaeological finds may be removed from Ireland only with the permission of the Irish government.

Law and Criminal Justice. Ireland is a parliamentary democracy. Its political and legal systems are strongly influenced by British traditions. Because it shares the same island with Northern Ireland, Ireland has in recent years been forced to contend with spill-over violence from the conflict in that country. Accordingly, the legislature has recently enacted special legislation giving the police enhanced powers when dealing with terrorism cases.

Ireland is a common law country, and the Irish criminal justice system functions in the common law tradition (as described in Section II;8) very much in the manner of the United Kingdom.

Illegal drugs are not a particularly prominent problem in Ireland, which may have somewhat conflicting consequences. In one sense the authorities do not have illegal drugs as high on their agenda of priorities. However, if caught in a drug offense, the individual may be treated more harshly than in countries where drugs are a more familiar problem.

---

7. ITALY

U.S. Embassy and Consulates.

Embassy and Consulate
Via Veneto 119/A
Rome
Tel. (6) 4674

Consular Office
Via Baccarini 1
Palermo
Tel. (91) 291-532 thru 5

Consular Office
Banca D'America e d'Italla Bldg.
Piazza Portello 6
Genoa
Tel. (10) 282-741 thru 5

Consular Office
Lungarmo Amerigo Vespucce 38
Florence
Tel. (55) 298-276

Consular Office
Piazza Repubblica 32
Milano
Tel. (2) 652-841 thru 5

Consular Office
Via Roma 9
Trieste
Tel. (40) 687-28 thru 29

Consular Office
Piazza della Republica
Naples
Tel. (81) 660-966

Passport and Visa Requirements for Incoming Americans. An American must have a valid passport to travel in Italy. If the duration of the stay is expected to be less than 90 days, no visa is required. Upon proper application, and proof that the applicant is a bona fide tourist with proper means of support, that 90-day period may be extended to 180 days total. A traveler wishing to make such application may do so at any police station (questura). When in the United States, inquiries and application should be addressed to the Italian consulates in this country (listed in Appendix C).

Residence. A traveler who plans to stay in Italy for a period in excess of 90 days is defined as a "resident" for purposes of Italy's immigration law and is required to obtain a resident visa. The traveler must:

- have a valid passport (and, if the applicant is an ex-Italian citizen, U.S. naturalization papers);
- complete an application form specifying, among other things, the reason for and the length and place of the stay in Italy;
- present evidence of self-sufficiency.

The application for a resident visa should be made before going to Italy at an Italian consulate in this country. Action on the application requires the approval of several ministries in Rome and therefore may take many weeks to clear.

Employment. Americans desiring to work in Italy must obtain a work permit and employment visa. Note that the Italian government has warned that "the time necessary to receive authorization from Italy can vary from three months to one year." The traveler must, therefore, take care to make arrangements sufficiently far in advance.

In order to obtain a work permit and visa, the employer must first obtain permission from the Ministry of Labor. Once that permit is granted, the individual must apply for a work permit and visa at an Italian consulate in this country. The authorities will require:

- valid passport (and, if the applicant is an ex-Italian citizen, a U.S. naturalization paper);
- an application form, specifying, among other things, the applicant's capacity to provide for return travel from Italy when the permit expires;
- clearance from the local police officials.

The Italians also have a separate visa for foreigners desiring to engage in work, not as an employee, but independently, such as a professional person or self-employed businessperson. The application process is essentially the same (except, of course, no permit from an employer is necessary).

Americans desiring to find work in Italy must heed the following warning from the American consulate: "It is usually very difficult for Americans to find jobs in Italy, whether professional, clerical, skilled, unskilled, full-time or part-time....Americans are urged not to come to Italy with the hope of finding work unless they have a firm employment contract and the appropriate work permit issued by the Italian authorities." The fact is that the Italian government will not issue a work permit to a foreigner for any job for which an Italian is available and capable of performing. Because of high unemployment, there are many available Italians looking for work at every level of skill.

Study. Many Americans come to Italy to study, and though a student visa is necessary, it can be obtained with considerably less difficulty than permission for employment and residence. Application should be made at an Italian consulate in this country, which will require:

- a valid passport;
- an application that includes evidence that the student, or the student's parents, are financially capable of providing for the student while in Italy;
- a letter of acceptance from a school or university in Italy, with specifics regarding place, duration of courses, and dates of attendance.

Tourist Registration Requirements. All tourists in Italy must register with the police within three days of arrival in the country. Technically, even tourists staying in a hotal must register with the police, in person. However, as explained by the American consulate, that registration requirement "is usually waived if a tourist plans a short stay of one or two weeks and is staying in a hotel or the like." In such cases, the hotel management will routinely attend to this formality, and the traveler will be asked to surrender his or her passport for a short while so that registration may be arranged. However, a traveler staying in a private home or campgrounds must personally go to the nearest police station to register within that three-day period.

Customs Restrictions for Incoming Americans. American travelers arriving in Italy may bring into the country, duty-free, the following:

- tobacco—400 cigarettes and a quantity of cigars or pipe tobacco not exceeding 500 grams;
- wine—2 bottles;

- liquor—1 bottle;
- coffee—2 kilograms (4.4 lbs.);
- sugar—3 kilograms (6.6 lbs.);
- cocoa—1 kilogram (2.2 lbs.).

Personal effects, which are also admitted duty-free, include clothing (new and used), books, camping and household equipment, fishing tackle, one sporting gun and 200 cartridges, one pair of skis, two tennis racquets, portable typewriter, record player with ten records, tape recorder or dictaphone, baby carriage, two still cameras with ten rolls of film, one movie camera with ten rolls of film, binoculars, personal jewelry and portable radio (which may be subject to small license fee).

All such items may be admitted duty-free only on condition that they are for personal use and are not for sale, gift, or trade.

American travelers arriving in Italy after visiting other countries are allowed to carry into Italy, duty-free, gifts of up to a value of $500, including one-half liter of perfume.

Currency Regulations and Banking. There are no restrictions on the amount of foreign money currency that is imported into Italy. Because there are controls on the amount of currency that may be removed from Italy, people traveling with large quantities of currency are advised to declare such currency on entry. Such declaration then "establishes for the Italian Customs Office of Exit that the currency came from abroad and that, therefore, the same amount or less may be re-exported."

Italian currency in excess of 300,000 lire may not be either imported into, or exported from, Italy.

Dollars are freely convertible to lire at banks, as well as hotels, restaurants, etc. However, it is virtually impossible to cash a personal check drawn on an American bank, and it is not possible to open a lire account in an Italian bank unless the depositor is a legal resident in Italy.

The following are some of the American banks with branches in Italy:

Bank of America;
Banca d'America e d'Italia;
Via Borgogna 8
Milan
Tel. 77951

Largo Tritone, 161
Rome
Tel. 67181

Citibank, N.A.;
Foro Buonaparte N. 16
Milan
Tel. 85421

Via Boncompagni 26
Rome
Tel. 4713

Chemical Bank.
Largo Cairoli 2
Milan
Tel. 85801

The principal American Express offices are located at:

Piazza di Spagna 38
Rome
Tel. 6764

1471 San Moise (San Marco)
Venice
Tel. 700-844

19 Via Vittor Pisani
Milan
Tel. 670-9060

Check with American Express for a complete list of its facilities
throughout the country.

Health Requirements. No vaccinations are required to enter
Italy, and there are no special health problems for travelers in
Italy.

In an emergency, the following hospital has English-speaking staff:

Salvator Mundi Inernation Hospital,
Viale Mura Gianicolensi 67,
Rome
Tel. 586-041.

There are also many private clinics and hospitals throughout
Italy.

Americans in need of medical assistance should contact the
closest American consulate. The consulate will have a more
complete list of hospital facilities, as well as a list of English-
speaking doctors and health professionals. (See Section I:2
on U.S. consular services.) Americans should be aware, however, that the quality of public medical care in Italy is not comparable to that available in the United States (or most of Europe for that matter). One woman, traveling in Italy, told of
being given $500 by her father to hold in case she got sick, and
then to use the money to get out of Italy immediately. Horror
stories about the public hospitals in Italy are common and usually include descriptions such as "terrible" and "deplorable."
The only advisable thing to do, therefore, is not get sick in Italy;
and if you do, then at least stay away from the public medical

facilities. Find a private doctor, or a private clinic if necessary.

Automobile and Highway Regulations. Americans planning to drive in Italy should obtain an international driver's license before leaving the United States. However, an American license is valid in Italy if accompanied with a translation and a statement of validity, which can be obtained from the Italian Automobile Club (ACI), located at Via Cristoforo Colombo 261, Rome.

Driving in Italy is generally governed by rules of the road familiar to Americans. However, driving in Italian cities can be an experience for which most Americans will not be prepared. Small automobiles and cycles move through narrow streets in seemingly crazy disarray for which no rules can amend and no advice can prepare. All you can do is take it slowly.

Speed limits are typically 50 kilometers per hour (about 31 mph) in towns, 110 km/h (about 68 mph) on the open road, and 140 km/h (about 87 mph) on the highway.

The Italian Automobile Club (ACI) provides an emergency breakdown service that can be contacted by calling 116 throughout Italy. The ACI may also be contacted for driving information and assistance.

Art and Antiquities. For at least the last ten years the Italian authorities have been serious about attempting to prevent the removal of Italy's artistic and cultural treasures from the country. The export of art and antiquities is governed by national law that provides for government review of all art exports and for government purchase of that art if it is deemed of such cultural or artistic value that it should not be permitted to leave the country. For the most part, these legal provisions are invoked only with respect to the most extraordinary pieces of art and will have no impact on the purchases of the typical American traveler.

Law and Criminal Justice. Italy is a democratic republic with a parliamentary government. Since World War II, Italy has had a recurring and quite serious problem with political terrorism. In recent years, in part because of the effectiveness of the police, and probably also because of changes in the political atmosphere, the intensity and frequency of internal terrorism has diminished substantially. The police are therefore able to devote considerably more time to the investigation of organized crime, and particularly its drug business. Recent massive police arrests of organized crime leaders are big news in Italy, and in the United States.

Italy is a civil law country, and the Italian criminal justice system functions in the Continental tradition (as described in Section II;8). Among its particular attributes are the following:

- A person arrested is held incommunicado for as long as three days, pending completion of an interrogation by the prosecutor. During this period, foreign prisoners are not even permitted to speak with a consular official.

- That initial interrogation by the prosecutor must be conducted in the presence of the defense counsel; however, other than being present at the interrogation, even the defense counsel may not see the prisoner during this period.

- Italy is well known for the slow pace of its criminal justice system. It often takes many years before a trial is held — which can be an extreme hardship for any prisoner but is especially difficult for the foreigner, who may be incarcerated during the entire time.

- To accommodate that slow pace, Italian law permits unusually long periods of pretrial confinement. The permissible duration of pretrial confinement is keyed to the seriousness of the crime charged; obviously, the more serious the crime, the longer the prisoner may be jailed before trial. As of 1984, the maximum period of detention for the most serious offenses, from the time of arrest to the completion of the investigation, is three years. (Drug cases, again depending on seriousness, are typically half that length.) However, after the investigation is over, the accused may be held still longer until trial; and then again awaiting appeal. In 1985, a pretrial detention reform law should come into effect shortening the periods of permissible confinement. However, even under the new rules, prisoners in Italy will still be subject to among the longest pretrial confinement in Western Europe.

- Bail is rarely used in Italy. If the authorities deem it appropriate to release you pending trial, they will do so without bail; if they do not think release is warranted, then the ability to post bail will not help.

The recent police interest in organized crime has also elevated the priority of the police's focus on drug violations. For the most part, that interest is centered on the large-scale drug transactions of the professional trafficker, and those crimes are dealt with harshly.

---

8. L U X E M B O U R G
(The Grand Duchy of Luxembourg)

U.S. Embassy and Consulate.

Embassy and Consulate
22 Boulevard Emmanuel-Servais
Luxembourg
Tel. 401-23 thru 7.

Passport and Visa Requirements for Incoming Americans.
To enter Luxembourg, an American citizen needs a valid passport. No visa is required for a stay of three months or less. When in the United States, inquiries about extended stays in Luxembourg should be addressed to the Luxembourg consulates in this country (listed in Appendix C).

Employment. An American desiring to obtain employment in Luxembourg must obtain a work permit by submitting the following documents:

- a valid passport;
- an affidavit that the applicant has not been convicted of a crime;
- an offer of employment from the prospective employer.

An American in the United States can make application for a work permit at any Luxembourg consulate. If you are already in Luxembourg, the application can be submitted to the Administration de l'Emploi, 34 Avenue de la Porte-Neuve, Luxembourg.

Residence. Americans desiring to reside in Luxembourg for a period in excess of three months must obtain a residence visa. That visa will be issued only upon showing that the applicant has obtained a work permit or has independent means of support.

Application can be made at the Luxembourg consulate in this country, or, in Luxembourg, at the Ministry of Foreign Affairs, 5 Rue Notre-Dame.

Tourist Registration Requirements. There are no tourist registration requirements in Luxembourg.

Customs Restrictions for Incoming Americans. Personal effects, actually accompanying the traveler, may be admitted duty-free. These include clothes, underclothes, and toilet articles in the traveler's luggage.

In addition, the following objects will be admitted duty-free if they are "in use" (that is, purchased for personal use) and accompanying the traveler: two still and two nonprofessional movie cameras, with appropriate film and portable projectors; sports equipment, such as skis, tennis rackets, and fishing tackle (sporting guns may be admitted only with authorization from the Ministry of Justice); one musical instrument; one portable radio; one pair of binoculars; one portable typewriter; one tent and related camping equipment; one baby carriage; and one portable TV.

Any of the personal items listed above that do not personally accompany the traveler, or any items not listed that are needed by the traveler for personal use during the trip, may also be admitted duty-free subject to payment of a reimbursable deposit covering the full amount of the duty that would be charged if the items did not accompany the traveler upon departure from Luxembourg.

In addition to the personal effects exemption, American travelers may import the following additional items duty-free (the numbers in parentheses are the amounts that may be imported from countries belonging to the EEC; however, for purposes of these customs regulations, any article purchased in a duty-free shop in any country is deemed to have been purchased outside the EEC):

- tobacco—400 (300) cigarettes or 200 (150) cigarillos or 100 (75) cigars or 500 (400) grams of smoking tobacco; if mixed, proportionate amounts;

- liquor—1 (1.5) liter if spirits contain more than 22 percent alcohol by volume, or 2 (3) liters if spirits contain less than 22 percent alcohol by volume, or 2 (3) liters of sparkling wine; if mixed, proportionately equivalent amounts;

- wine—2 (4) liters plus 8 liters of nonsparkling Luxembourg wine;

- perfume—50 (75) grams of perfume and 0.25 (0.375) liters of cologne. (The duty-free allowance for tobacco, liquor, or wine is applicable only if traveler is over 17 years of age.) Any other items being carried for personal use or gifts, and not for commercial purposes, may be imported duty-free up to a total value of 2,000 francs (9,600).

Currency Regulations and Banking. There are no restrictions on bringing foreign or Luxembourg currency into or out of Luxembourg in any denominations.

Luxembourg, like Switzerland, is one of the banking centers of Western Europe. The country has a self-described "liberality...towards foreign capital," which means that secrecy is protected, and money restrictions and regulations are kept to a minimum. As a result, this tiny country hosts well over a hundred different banking institutions.

The following are some of the American banks with branches in Luxembourg:

16, Avenue Marie-Therese
P.O. Box 1373
Luxembourg
Tel. 442240

Bank of America International, S.A.
35 Boulevard Royal

Caisse Postale 435
Luxembourg
Tel. 20841

The principal American Express office is located at:

41 Avenue de la Liberte
Luxembourg
Tel. 489-9

Check with American Express for a complete list of its facilities throughout the country.

Health Requirements. There are no vaccination requirements for entering Luxembourg.

Americans in need of medical assistance should contact the closest American consulate. The consulate will have a more complete list of hospital facilities, as well as a list of English-speaking doctors and health professionals. (See Section I:2 on U.S. consular services.)

Automobile and Highway Regulations. Americans are permitted to drive in Luxembourg with a valid U.S. driver's license for a maximum of three months. However, the driver must be at least 18 years old.

Driving in Luxembourg is generally governed by rules of the road familiar to Americans. Note, however, the following special rules:

- seat belts are mandatory for passengers in the front seat;
- the use of the car horn is prohibited in traffic congestion and may be used only in cases of imminent danger.

Speed limits are typically 60 kilometers per hour (about 37 mph) in towns, 90 km/h (about 56 mph) on the open road, and 120 km/h (about 74 mph) on the highway.

Law and Criminal Justice. Luxembourg is governed by a constitutional monarchy and a democratically elected parliament. Since the war, Luxembourg has been politically stable and free from much of the terrorist violence that has plagued the countries around it.

Luxembourg is a civil law country, and the Luxembourg criminal justice system functions in the Continental tradition (as described in Section II:8). Among its particular attributes is the following:

- After an arrest a person may be interrogated by the police for only 24 hours before being presented to a judge for a determination of whether further pretrial incarceration is permissible.

Luxembourg is not considered one of the drug centers of the continent, and it has not had a significant drug problem. However, possession of even relatively small quantities of hard drugs, even if for personal use, is treated as a serious crime likely to result in imprisonment.

---

9. THE NETHERLANDS (Holland)

Embassy
Lange Voorhout 102
The Hague
Tel. (070) 62-49-11

Consular Office
Baan 50
Rotterdam
Tel. (010) 11-75-60
(no consular services)

Consular Office
Museumplein 19
Amsterdam
Tel. (010) 79-03-21

Passport and Visa Requirements for Incoming Americans. In order to enter the Netherlands, a U.S. citizen must have a valid U.S. passport. (In addition, the traveler must technically also have sufficient funds to cover all expenses during the stay in the Netherlands and a departure ticket to a destination other than Belgium or Luxembourg, although the authorities will not usually check.) If the intended stay in the Netherlands is less than three months, no visa is required. When in the United States, inquiries and applications for extended stays in the Netherlands should be addressed to the Dutch consulates in this country (listed in Appendix C).

Residence. An American desiring to stay in the Netherlands longer than three months must report in person to the Alien Section of the local police department (vreemdelingenpolitie) to apply for either a temporary permit or a permanent residence permit.

Employment. In order to obtain employment in the Netherlands, an American must first complete the "application for residence permit" in a consulate in the United States. The employer must then apply for an employment permit to the Regional Office for Labour of the Minister of Social Affairs in the Netherlands. The government warns: "Only after having received this notification (that the work permit has been granted) should the person concerned leave for the Netherlands."

Note, however, that permission to work in the Netherlands will usually be given only to foreigners having special skills not otherwise available in the local labor pool.

Tourist Registration Requirements. There are no tourist registration requirements in the Netherlands.

Customs Restrictions for Incoming Americans. An American may bring all personal luggage into the Netherlands duty-free, even if the luggage is shipped to the Netherlands separately. If the amount or value of the goods included within personal luggage is "unusual," the traveler may be required to leave a deposit against the duty that will be assessed if the items in question are not taken from the Netherlands with the traveler upon departure.

Americans may also import the following items into the Netherlands duty-free (numbers in parentheses refer to amounts that may be imported from countries belonging to the EEC; however, for purposes of these customs regulations, any article purchased in a duty-free shop in any country is deemed to have been purchased outside the EEC):

- tobacco—400 (300) cigarettes or 200 (150) cigarillos or 100 (75) cigars or 500 (400) grams of tobacco;
- liquor—1 (1.5) liter if more than 22 percent alcohol by volume, or 2 (3) liters if less than 22 percent alcohol by volume, or 2 (3) liters of sparkling wine;
- wine—2 (4) liters and 8 liters of Luxembourg wine;
- perfume—50 (75) grams of perfume and 0.25 (0.375) liters of cologne;
- coffee—200 (750) grams of coffee or 100 (300) grams of instant coffee;
- tea—100 (150) grams of tea.

(The duty-free allowance for tobacco, liquor, or wine is applicable only if the traveler is over 17 years of age, and 15 years of age for coffee.) In addition, any other items may be brought into the Netherlands duty-free up to a value Fl. 700 for articles purchased in Belgium or Luxembourg, Fl. 540 for articles purchased in another EEC country and Fl. 125 for articles purchased in any other country. (For purposes of this provision, articles purchased in duty-free shops will be valued as if purchased outside the EEC.) Note: In the Netherlands, duty is not payable on amounts in excess of the foregoing limits if the items in question are re-exported within six months of entry.

Currency Regulations and Banking. There are no restrictions on bringing currency into or out of the Netherlands.

The following are some of the American banks with branches in the Netherlands:

>   Bank of America
>   Keizersgracht 617-629
>   P.O. Box 1638
>   Amsterdam
>   Tel. 21-46-21
>
>   Citibank
>   Herengracht 545-549
>   P.O. Box 2055
>   Amsterdam
>   Tel 26-44-55

The principal American Express offices are located at:

>   Damrak 66
>   Box 762
>   Tel. 26-20-42
>
>   Venestraat 20
>   The Hague
>   Tel. 46-95-15

Check with American Express for a complete list of its facilities throughout the country.

Health and Hospitals. There are no health requirements for entering the Netherlands from any country.

Americans in need of medical assistance should contact the closest American consulate. The consulate will have a more complete list of hospital facilities, as well as a list of English-speaking doctors and health professionals. (See Section I:2 on U.S. consular services.)

Automobile and Highway Regulations. American travelers may drive in the Netherlands using either an international driver's license or a valid American license.

Driving in the Netherlands is generally governed by rules of the road familiar to Americans. Americans should, however, note the following special rules: the driver and front seat passengers must wear seat belts; children under 12 may not ride in the front seat unless properly restrained in a car seat. In addition, drivers in the Netherlands must be very careful of bicyclists, who are more abundant in the Netherlands than perhaps in any other country. For the automobile driver, bicyclists are a particular hazard because they make unexpected turns and otherwise disregard normal traffic rules.

Speed limits are typically 50 kilometers per hour (about 37 mph) in towns, 80 km/h (about 49 mph) on the open road, and 100 km/h (about 62 mph) on the highway.

The Netherlands has two automobile clubs that can be contacted for assistance and information:

> Koninklijke Nederlandsche Toeristenbond ASWB
> Royoa Netherlands Touring Club
> 220 Wassenaarsweg
> The Hague

> Koninklijke Nederlansche Automobiel Club
> Royal Dutch Automobile Club
> 4 Sophialaan
> The Hague

In addition to the main offices, both clubs have branches around the country.

Law and Criminal Justice. The Netherlands is a constitutional monarchy with a democratic parliamentary government. In many respects, the Netherlands is considered to be one of the most "liberal" of the Western European countries—it is progressive in human affairs and restrictive of governmental intrusiveness.

The Netherlands is a civil law country, and the Dutch criminal justice system functions in the Continental tradition (as described in Section II;8). Among its particular attributes are the following:

- A person cannot be held by the police for interrogation for more than six hours. After that period elapses, the individual must be brought before a public prosecutor who may authorize further detention for an additional 48 hours. The prisoner must then be brought before a Judge of Instruction.

- The Judge of Instruction determines, among other things, whether further pretrial detention is warranted. The general preference in the Netherlands is to release the prisoner while awaiting trial. However, where specific circumstances indicate the probability that the defendant will not appear for trial, the judge may refuse release. This consideration may be applied to foreigners.

- Although bail is technically available, it is very rarely used.

95

1 0. PORTUGAL

U.S. Embassy and Consulates.

Embassy and Consulate
Avenida das Forcas Armadas
Lisbon
Tel. 72-56-00

Consular Office
Avenida D. Henrique
Ponta Delgada
Sao Miguel, Azores
Tel. 22216 and 7

Consular Office
Apartado No. 88
Rua Julio Dinis 826
Oporto
Tel. 6-3094 thru 6.

Passports and Visa Requirements for Incoming Americans. An American citizen must have a valid U.S. passport to enter Portugal. If traveling as a tourist, or on business, for a stay of up to 60 days, no visa is required. That 60-day limit may be extended monthly at the Visitors' Registration Service (*Seccao de Estrangeiros*) or at local police offices (*Policia de Seguranca Publica*), for a maximum stay of up to six months.

When the traveler is in Portugal, all visa applications and residence information should be addressed to the Foreigners' Registration Service, or its regional offices throughout the country. The address of the Foreigners' Registration Service in Lisbon is Avenida Antonio Augusto Aguiar 18, 1000 Lisboa (tel. 55-40-47). In the United States, inquiries and applications should be addressed to the Portuguese consulates in this country (listed in Appendix C).

Residence. An American desiring to stay in Portugal longer than six months must obtain a residence visa (authorization for residence). To obtain such a visa an American must submit the following documents to the appropriate Portuguese authorities:

• a valid passport;
• references from two Portuguese residents;
• detailed documentation of financial ability to provide for personal needs while in Portugal;
• a description of the activities expected to be engaged in while in the country;

- a police report from the traveler's place of residence in the United States reflecting the lack of any criminal record.

The government recommends that residence visa applications be submitted at least four months in advance of the intended departure from the United States.

Employment. Americans desiring to work in Portugal must first obtain a work permit, then a residence visa. The work permit is obtained by the prospective employer through application to local labor authorities. The Portuguese consulate is advised when the permit is granted and the individual may then rely on the permit in applying for a residence visa.

However, be advised that Portugal has been suffering a high rate of unemployment because of general economic difficulties, as well as the return of many Portuguese from other countries, and from Portugal's former colonies in Africa. Therefore, the American consulate warns: "Under these conditions, work permits for foreigners are especially difficult to obtain."

The best opportunity for Americans to obtain employment in Portugal is with U.S. corporations doing business there, and the American would be well advised to search and apply for those jobs while still in the United States.

Tourist Registration Requirements. There are no tourist registration requirements in Portugal.

Customs Restrictions for Incoming Americans. American tourists and other travellers without a residence visa may import, without duty:

- tobacco—250 grams (approximately 200 cigarettes, or 100 cigarillos, or 50 cigars);
- wine—2 liters;
- liquor—1 liter;
- perfume—liter;
- medicines—such as are required for personal use on the journey;
- personal belongings—clothing and articles for personal use (such as camera, radio and tape recorder, baby carriage, sports equipment, etc.) if such articles "show clearly" that they are used and are included in the traveler's luggage.

Portuguese authorities specifically warn: "Passengers who have in their luggage any articles which, owing to their quantity or quality, are presumed to be intended for sale are subject not only to payment of import duty and taxes, but also to a fine."

Currency Regulations and Banking. On entering the country, American travelers may bring with them up to 5,000 escudos. There is no limit on the amount of bank or traveler's checks in escudos that may be brought into the country. There is also no limit on the amount of foreign currency or bank and traveler's checks that may be brought into the country.

On leaving Portugal, an American may take out:

- 5,000 escudos per person (at least 18 years old);
- an amount equal to 70,000 escudos in foreign currency per person (at least 18 years old), except if the traveler can prove a larger amount of currency was brought into the country by that person. (Thus, travelers with large amounts of currency may wish to declare and register it with customs upon arrival in order to avoid customs difficulties on departure);
- bank and traveler's checks in any amount if issued outside of Portugal in the traveler's name.

Currency can be exchanged only at banks and official exchange facilities at airports, border crossings, and tourist resorts. Only some hotels are authorized to exchange currency. The rate of exchange is always the official rate and is the same everywhere.

There are no American banks that have branches in Portugal and the "correspondent" banks of the American banks will not provide cash advances on the major American bank credit cards. However, lost or stolen credit cards—including Master-Card, Visa, Diners Club and Carte Blanche (but not American Express) —can be reported to:

Unibanco
Praco D. Joao da Camara
Lisbon
Tel. 32-80-26 or 37-27-68

The American Express Office is located at:

The STAR Agency
Avenida Sidonio Pais
Lisbon
Tel. 53-98-41

Check with American Express for a complete list of its facilities throughout the country. Note that because of restrictive local banking regulations, the agency representing American Express in Lisbon is not a full banking facility and therefore cannot provide all of the financial services that American Express makes available elsewhere.

Health and Hospitals. There are no vaccination or other special health requirements for Americans, except that travelers who have come from, or passed through, regions of the world experiencing cholera or smallpox epidemics will be admitted only with an international certificate of vaccination against such diseases. In addition, travelers coming from Central or South America or equatorial Africa who are going to Madeira or the Azores will be admitted only with an international certificate of vaccination against yellow fever.

There is no American hospital in Portugal. There is a small British hospital—Hospital Ingles, located at Rua Saraiva de Carvalho, 49, Lisboa (tel. 60-20-20) —where the staff speaks English. The British hospital does not treat emergencies, but does have a clinic open weekdays.

Some of the emergency medical facilities are:

Hospital da CUF
Travessa do Castro, 3
Lisboa
Tel. 60-91-11

Hospital Julio de Matos
(Health Emergencies)
Avenida do Brazil
Lisboa
Lisboa Tel. 77-11-41

Hospital Particular
Avenida uis Bivar, 30
Lisboa
Tel. 53-90-31

Hospital de Cascais
Rua D. Francisco de Avilez
Cascais
Tel. 286-0971

Americans in need of medical assistance should contact the closest American consulate. The consulate will have a more complete list of hospital facilities, as well as a list of English-speaking doctors and health professionals. (See Section I:2 on U.S. consular services.)

Automobile and Highway Regulations. In order to be permitted to drive, an American must have an international driver's license.

Driving in Portugal is generally governed by rules of the road familiar to Americans. In addition, Portugal strictly enforces a priority for cars coming from the right (except for cars entering major highways). Portugal requires that seat belts be worn, if available in the car. It is also mandatory that the car be equipped with an International Warning Triangle, which must be used if the car breaks down.

Speed limits are typically 60 kilometers per hour (about 37

mph) in towns, 90 km/h (about 56 mph) on the open road, and 120 km/h (about 74 mph) on the highway.

In the event of a breakdown, the Automobile Club of Portugal (*Automovel Club de Portugal* or ACP) has an emergency service. The northern region, as far as Figueira da Foz, is handled by the Oporto network, which can be contacted at tel. 29-271/2/3. The southern region is covered by the Lisboa network at tel. 77-54-75, 77-54-02, and 77-54-91. The main office of the ACP which, along with its regional offices throughout the country, can be contacted for automobile touring information, is located at Rua Tosa Araujo 24, 1200 Lisboa (tel. 56-39-31).

Art and Antiquities. Portuguese law requires that the export of anything of significant value, including art and antiquities, as well as gold, silver and jewelry, must be approved by government authorities. The export application (*Boletim de Registo de Exportacao*) is available from:

> Ministerio da Economia
> Rua Nova de Sao Mamede 76
> Lisbon

Law and Criminal Justice. Portugal today is a multiparty parliamentary democracy in which the government is appointed by the president and serves only with the support of the parliament. As late as 1974, Portugal was ruled by a military dictatorship that had grown ever more repressive, and correspondingly unpopular, during its 50-year reign of power. Since 1974, however, as a result of increasing criticism of the military's policies, there has been a steady transition from authoritarian to democratic government. In fact, in the last decade, Portugal has had two major constitutional revisions, in 1976 and 1982, that have successively established and reinforced the basic protections of due process of law and civil liberties.

Portugal is a civil law country, and the Portuguese criminal justice system functions in the Continental tradition (as described in Section II:8). Among its particular attributes are the following:

- The initial period of confinement, before being brought before a judge, is 48 hours. However, upon authorization of the judge and depending on the seriousness of the crime, a prisoner may be kept for a total of three years before trial (and even longer in some circumstances of multiple violations) in preventive detention.

- Provisional liberty will not be granted, and bail may not be posted, for prisoners accused of certain crimes. These include most serious violent crimes, such as assault on the life of another, as well as robbery, check fraud, illegal weapons violations, and the "production, selling, transport and possession of illicit drugs."

- Although most prisoners are not kept in pretrial detention for the full legal limit, the Portuguese criminal system is slow, and long waits of many months before trial is scheduled are not uncommon.

- Portuguese law does provide for a jury trial, but only for the most serious offenses. Interestingly, the trial-by-jury requirements have only recently been incorporated into Portuguese law by the 1982 Constitution, and so it is not yet in wide use.

- Plea-bargaining is not accepted in any sense in this country. As stated by the office of the Ministerio da Justica, "Under Portuguese law the objective of the penal process can not be dispensed with; it is not subject to negotiation between the parties...it is not possible to withdraw charges; agreements between the prosecution and the defense are not valid; and no limitations can be imposed on the court in its consideration of a case brought to trial."

- Although Portuguese prisoners are treated humanely, Portuguese prisons are generally old and in very poor condition.

Generally, Americans travel to Portugal for a vacation on the quiet side, rather than a raucous, swinging time, and so they tend not to get into a great deal of trouble. The only serious problem for Americans is drug smuggling, either for business or personal purposes.

Portugal is just north of, and a common transit stop from, Morocco, where illegal drugs—particularly hashish and marijuana—are abundantly available. In order to interdict the flow of drugs from Morocco through Portugal to the United States, the United States has urged Portugal to "take vigorous action" against traffickers. Consequently, particularly on African routes, the Portuguese authorities maintain a careful watch and Portugal has recently increased the penalty for the most serious drug-trafficking offenses.

11. SPAIN

U.S. Embassy and Consulates.

Embassy and Consulate
Serrano 75
Madrid
Tel. 276-3400

Consular Office
Paseo de las Delicias No. 7
Seville
Tel. 23-1885

Consular Office
Via Layetana 33
Barcelona
Tel. 319-09550

Consular Office
Avenida del Ejercito, 11
Bilbao
Tel. 435-8308/9.

Passport and Visa Requirements for Incoming Americans. An American must have a valid passport to visit Spain. Entry will be permitted for a period of three months without a visa. In the United States, inquiries about the visa requirements for extended stays in Spain should be addressed to the Spanish consulates in this country (listed in Appendix C).

Employment. A person who intends to work in Spain must show that the employer has signed a contract for the foreign labor and that the employment arrangement has been "legalized" by the Ministry of Labor in Spain (*Delegacion Provincial de Trabajo*). However, it is very difficult for an American to get a job in Spain. Unemployment is high for Spaniards; American businesses in Spain are required to hire Spaniards to the greatest extent possible (in fact, the consulate advises that American businesses have specifically requested that the consulate not even mention their names to prospective job-hunters), and they rarely hire Americans except, perhaps, as experienced executives.

Study. A person who intends to study in Spain must present evidence of enrollment in a school and proof of sources of income while in Spain.

Residence. An American desiring to stay in Spain for more than three months may obtain a special visa for extended stay at any Spanish consulate in this country upon presentation of a valid passport and two passport-size pictures. Alternatively, if the American is in Spain when deciding to stay, the permission for extension (permiso de permanencia) may be obtained by applying at the police station in the district where the American is residing. In Madrid, that permission may be obtained at the Jefatura Superior de Policia, Los Madrazo 9, Madrid (tel. 221 2525).

Tourist Registration Requirements. There are no tourist registration requirements in Spain for the traveler staying less than three months. Thereafter, the traveler should register with the local police.

Customs Restrictions for Incoming Americans. Americans visiting Spain may bring into the country, duty-free, all personal effects (articles which the traveler reasonably needs, taking into account the circumstances of the trip; personal articles may not include any merchandise for commercial purposes). All such personal effects must be re-exported from Spain upon the traveler's departure.

Personal effects include wearing apparel, jewelry, toilet articles, two still and one movie camera (each with ten rolls of film), a pair of binoculars, a musical instrument, a record player, a portable radio and TV, a tape recorder, a portable typewriter, and sports equipment for personal use (including two sport rifles and 100 cartridges per rifle).

In some cases, when the items being brought into the country are new or especially valuable, the Spanish customs authorities will insist on a deposit against, or guarantee of, the import duties that would be due if the articles in question were not re-exported with the traveler. This deposit or guarantee will be returned when the traveler leaves the country with the goods.

In addition to the personal effects exemption, American travelers may import the following additional items duty-free:

- tobacco—400 cigarettes or 100 cigars or 500 grams of tobacco;
- liquor—1 liter if greater than 22 percent alcohol, 2 liters if equal to or less than 22 percent alcohol;
- wine—2 liters;
- perfume—50 grams;
- cologne—0.25 liters.

(The duty-free allowance for tobacco, liquor, or wine is applicable only if the traveler is over 15 years of age.)

Currency Regulations and Banking. Americans traveling to Spain may import foreign currency without limitation. However, no more than 200,000 pesetas in Spanish currency may be imported.

When leaving the country, a traveler may not take out more than 20,000 pesetas in Spanish currency.

The following are some of the American banks with branches in Spain:

Chemical Bank;
36/38 Passeo de la Castellana
Madrid
Tel. 431-2500

Bank of America, S.A.E.;
Calle del Capitan Haya 1
Madrid
Tel. 455-5500

Citibank, N.A.;
Jose Ortega y Gasset 29
Madrid
Tel. 404-3015

The principal American Express offices are located at:

Plaza de las Cortes No. 2
Madrid
Tel. 222-1180

Paseo de Gracia
Chaflan Rosellon
Barcelona
Tel. 218-6712

Check with American Express for a complete list of its facilities throughout the country.

Health and Hospitals. There are no special health requirements for entering Spain. The only serious medical problem frequently encountered in Spain is a gastrointestinal upset (commonly known by such vividly descriptive names as "Montezuma's Revenge," or simply "The Turistas"). The American consulate's Health and Medical Information Sheet warns: "The drinking water is safe in Madrid, however, bottled water is recommended for travelers." Therefore, Americans intending to travel around Spain should come well supplied with appropriate medication, such as Pepto-Bismol, which may be in short supply in the countryside.

There is a British-American hospital in Madrid which has an English-speaking staff and handles emergencies. It is at:

Paseo de Juan XXIII, 1,
Ciudad Universitaria,
Madrid,
(Tel. 233-31-00).

Americans in need of medical assistance should contact the closest American consulate. The consulate will have a more complete list of hospital facilities, as well as a list of English-speaking doctors and health professionals. (See Section I:2 on U.S. consular services.)

Automobile and Highway Regulations. An American traveler desiring to drive in Spain must have:

- an international driver's license issued outside Spain, or
- a valid American driver's license, with a Spanish translation, and notarized by the American consulate in Spain or the Royal Automobile Club of Spain.

Driving in Spain is generally governed by rules of the road familiar to Americans.

Speed limits are typically 60 kilometers per hour (about 37 mph) in towns; 90 km/h (about 56 mph) on the open road; and 120 km/h (about 74 mph) on the highway.

The Royal Automobile Club, located at Jose Abascal 10, Madrid, may be consulted for information and assistance.

Law and Criminal Justice. Spain is a parliamentary democracy functioning under a constitutional monarchy. The democratic tradition in Spain, though flourishing today, is only about a decade old. For approximately the preceding 40 years, the country was governed under the dictatorship of Gen. Francisco Franco. Spain has emerged from the political and social repression of Franco's rule with a new libertarian constitution and an encouraging tolerance for diversity.

Spain is a civil law country, and the Spanish criminal justice system functions in the Continental tradition (as described in Section II:8). Among its particular attributes are the following:

- After an arrest, every prisoner must be brought before a judge within 72 hours. The judge will then determine whether there is sufficient reason to keep the prisoner in pretrial confinement. In addition, a prisoner may be held incommunicado for up to five days (and three days longer in very serious cases), although defense counsel will have access to the prisoner.
- The maximum period of pretrial confinement depends on the seriousness of the crime charged, and ranges from 6 months to 18 months. (At the time of publication, measures were pending to extend that range up to four years.)
- Generally, criminal trials occur between nine months and one year after the arrest.
- Spain does not have a jury system.
- There is no plea-bargaining in Spain at all.

The drug laws of Spain are unusual in this respect: the possession of any drug, solely for personal use, is not illegal. However, the transfer of any drug, even to a spouse, for example, and even if no money is involved, is illegal. Trafficking offenses are assessed on whether the drug is seriously harmful to the public health; possession of the less harmful soft drugs is not punished harshly (although a prison term is likely for significant amounts), but the most harmful hard drugs are punished much more severely. Aggravating circumstances—such as trafficking for an organized crime operation—increases that punishment substantially.

1 2. S W I T Z E R L A N D

U.S. Embassy and Consulates.

Embassy and Consulate
Jubllaeumstrasse 93
Bern
Tel. (031) 437-011

Consular Office
Zollikerstrasse 141
Zurich
Tel. (01) 552-566

Consular Office
11, Route de Pregny
Chambesy/Geneva
Tel. (022) 990-211

Passport and Visa Requirements for Incoming Americans.
American citizens must have a valid passport to visit Switzerland. No visa is required as long as the traveler does not engage in any "gainful activities," and stays in Switzerland less than three months. A traveler may extend that three-month limitation by applying at the nearest police station. When in the United States, inquiries and applications should be addressed to the Swiss consulates in this country (listed in Appendix C).

Employment. Americans who wish to work in Switzerland must obtain a visa before arriving in the country. The government warns: "Authorization to work is usually denied to tourists who seek employment after their arrival." Under Swiss law, the employer must apply for the necessary work permit from both the federal and cantonal (state) Foreigner's Police. Processing usually takes many months. If the permit is granted, one then apply for a visa at any Swiss consulate.

The Swiss government makes a point of emphasizing that "the rapid increase of foreigners has compelled the Federal Government to take measures designed to stem the influx of foreign labor and it is difficult to obtain the necessary work permit." Before granting any permits for the employment of foreigners, the government must be satisfied that there are no qualified Swiss citizens available for the job. And even then, the number of non-Swiss employees who may be hired by any business in Switzerland is strictly controlled by the authorities. In addition, Americans frequently are further disadvantaged by the fact that Switzerland is multilingual, and many jobs require fluency in more than one language.

Residence. Americans who wish to live in Switzerland on a long-term basis, even if they do not seek employment, must obtain a residence visa. Application forms may be obtained at Swiss consulates and must be submitted along with documentary evidence of financial resources sufficient to defray expenses, a statement of personal history (curriculum vitae or resume), and two passport photographs. Permission to receive a residence visa must be obtained directly from Switzerland, so the process may be somewhat time-consuming.

Tourist Registration Requirements. Switzerland does not have any tourist registration requirement.

Customs Restrictions for Incoming Americans. American travelers may bring into Switzerland, duty-free, all personal effects including clothing, toilet articles, sports equipment, and amateur photographic equipment and films.

Americans may also import the following items duty-free (numbers in parentheses refer to amounts that may be imported when entering from a European country):

- liquor—2 liters (if 15 proof or less), 1 liter (if over 15 proof);
- tobacco—400 (200) cigarettes or 100 (50) cigars or 500 (250) grams of tobacco. (The duty free allowance for liquor or tobacco is applicable only if traveler is over 17 years of age.) Goods imported for gift purposes (with the exception of meat, butter or "quantities of goods intended to be laid in store") may be imported duty-free up to a total of 100 Sfr. (Those under 17 have a limit of 50 Sfr.) In addition, each person entering the country is granted a 50 Sfr. exemption from duty for goods brought into Switzerland.

Currency Regulations and Banking. Swiss and foreign currency may be imported and exported without restriction.

As everyone knows, Switzerland is one of the world's great banking centers, and the major cities are full of banks.

The following are some of the American banks with branches in Switzerland:

Chemical Bank;
8 Rue Kleberg
Geneva
Tel. 31 24 07

Freigutstrasse 16
Zurich
Tel. 201 0440

Citibank, N.A.;
16 Quai General Guisan
Geneva
Tel. 20 55 16

Seestrasse 25
Zurich
Tel. 205 7111

Bank of America, N.T. & S.A.
15 Rue Du General DuFour
Geneva
Tel. 21 89 33

Bleicherweg 15
Zurich
Tel. 205 5111

The principal American Express offices are located at:

7 Rue Du Mont Blanc
Geneva
Tel. 317-600

Marktgasse 37
Bern
Tel. 23-66-90

Bahnhofstrasse 20
Zurich
Tel. 211-8370

Check with American Express for a complete list of its facilities throughout the country.

Health and Hospitals. Vaccinations are not required for entry into Switzerland.

Switzerland has excellent medical services and facilities. In the event of medical emergency, the American consulates have listings of hospitals and English-speaking doctors.

Note: Emergency medical assistance is available by calling the number 117 from any telephone in Switzerland.

Automobile and Highway Regulations. An American driver's license is valid in Switzerland, but only if the American is at least 18 years old. Driving in Switzerland is governed by rules of the road familiar to most Americans. Of particular interest to American drivers in Switzerland are rules requiring that:

- headlights be dimmed when driving through tunnels;
- passing on the right is strictly prohibited;
- seat belts must be worn when driving;
- children under 12 may not travel in the front seat.

Speed limits are typically 60 kilometers per hour (about 37 mph) in towns; 110 km/h (about 62 mph) on the open road; and 130 km/h (about 81 mph) on the highway.

There are two Swiss automobile clubs, which are both available for automobile information and assistance:

> Swiss Automobile Club
> (Automobil-Club der Schweiz)
> 9 Rue Pierre-Fatio
> Bern
>
> Swiss Touring Club
> (Touring Club Suisse)
> Wasserwerkgasse 39
> Geneva

A motorist in need of road assistance may call 140 throughout the country. Mountain roads are generally equipped with emergency call boxes.

Art and Antiquities. There are no controls on the export of art from Switzerland.

Law and Criminal Justice. Switzerland is a republic, consisting of 25 federated states (most are called cantons, and some are called half-cantons). In structure, the Swiss Confederation is akin to our own system of federal and state sovereignty. In Switzerland, the central government is granted certain limited powers and all remaining powers rest with the cantons, including a great deal of control over the operation of the criminal justice system. Therefore, generalizations are difficult. However, Switzerland is a civil law country, and the Swiss criminal justice system functions within the general scope of the Continental tradition (as described in Section II:8). Among its particular attributes are the following:

- The Swiss do have a jury system, but only for major crimes such as murder. Most crimes are tried by a panel of three judges, although minor cases may be presented before a single judge.

- After arrest, the suspect may be held for between 24 and 48 hours (depending on the canton) before being brought before a judge to determine whether further pretrial incarceration is appropriate.

- Bail is an accepted, but generally not common, practice (except in Geneva, where it is used regularly). However, bail will likely not be deemed a sufficient motivation to stay in Switzerland and therefore may not be granted to a foreigner unless there are some other ties to the country.

- Switzerland has a record of bringing suspects swiftly to trial, usually within months of the arrest; a one-year delay would be considered extraordinary.

Over the years, Switzerland's drug laws have been tightened and the resulting penalties made increasingly severe for serious violations, which are considered cases where the defendant is a member of a criminal organization or where the defendant has made large illicit profits or where the quantity of drugs endangers the health of many people.

13. UNITED KINGDOM
(England and Northern Ireland)

U.S. Embassy and Consulates.

Embassy and Consulate
24/44 Grosvenor Square
London, England
Tel. (01) 499-9000

Consular Office
Queen's House
14 Queen Street
Belfast, Northern Ireland

Passport and Visa Requirements for Incoming Americans.
An American traveler must have a passport to enter the United Kingdom. Generally, admission without a visa will be permitted for a period of six months, although that period may be extended to as much as a year. However, travelers admitted as tourists must be able to prove that they are financially able to cover their expenses and the cost of leaving the United Kingdom.

A traveler in the United Kingdom who wishes to make arrangements for an extended stay as a tourist should write to the British Immigration and Nationality Department, Lunar House, Wellesley Road, Croydon CR9, 2BY. The letter should include an explanation for extending the stay, as well as evidence of the traveler's ability to provide for accommodations and other expenses. In the United States, inquiries and applications should be addressed to the British consulates in this country (listed in Appendix C).

Study. Americans desiring to study in the United Kingdom must obtain entry clearance either from a British consulate before going to the United Kingdom or from the Home Office (Lunar House, Wellesley Road, Croydon CR9, 2BY) if already in the United Kingdom. Entry clearance will be granted only upon a proper showing that the individual has been accepted for a course of study and that the individual is able to pay the necessary tuition and living expenses.

Employment. An American must have a work permit in order to hold a job in the United Kingdom. The prospective employer is required to obtain the work permit by applying to the Department of Employment, Foreign Labor Section, Ebury Bridge House, Ebury Bridge Road, London SWl. Once the permit is granted, the employer sends it to the employee, who may then come to the United Kingdom and present the permit upon entry at the immigration check.

Generally, work permits will be issued only when there are no available British workers in the following categories: professionals, executives, highly specialized technicians, and key workers with special expertise or skills. Note that an American must be outside the United Kingdom in order for the work permit application to be processed. Therefore, the traveler should not come to the United Kingdom as a tourist hoping to find a job and change status while in the country.

The United Kingdom has established certain "permit-free" categories of workers who do not need a work permit to obtain employment in the United Kingdom. (However, even permit-free workers must obtain entry clearance, which will usually be granted only upon a showing that the individual is financially able to pay all expenses without recourse to public funds.) These include, among others, ministers of religion and other clergy, representatives of a foreign business that does not have a branch in the United Kingdom, members of the press and media, doctors and dentists, operational staff of non-British airlines, and artists and writers.

Tourist Registration Requirements. Americans who have been granted permission, for any reason, to stay in the United Kingdom for longer than six months must register with the police.

In London this can be done at the Aliens Registration Office in Lambs Conduit Street, London WCIN 3NX. A registration fee and two passport-size photographs are required. Outside London, registration can be accomplished at the local police station.

111

Changes in address or immigration status must also be reported to the authorities within seven days.

Customs Restrictions for Incoming Americans. Travelers may import, duty-free, all personal effects in their possession when entering the United Kingdom.

In addition, American travelers may import the following items duty-free (the numbers in parentheses are the amounts that may be imported from countries belonging to the EEC; however, for purposes of these customs regulations, any article purchased in a duty-free shop in any country is deemed to have been purchased outside the EEC):

- tobacco—400 (300) cigarettes or 200 (150) cigarillos or 100 (75) cigars or 500 (400) grams of smoking tobacco;

- liquor—1 (1.5) liter if spirits contain more than 22 percent alcohol by volume, or 2 (3) liters if spirits contain less than 22 percent alcohol by volume, or 2 (3) liters of sparkling wine;

- perfume—50 (75) grams of perfume and 0.25 (0.375) liters of cologne.

(The duty-free allowances for tobacco, liquor or wine is applicable only if traveler is over 17 years of age.) Any other items not being carried for commercial purposes may be imported duty-free up to a total value of L28 (L120).

Currency Regulations and Banking. There are no restrictions on bringing currency into, or taking currency out of, the United Kingdom.

The following are some of the American banks with branches in England:

Bank of America;
1 Watling Street
P.O. Box 262
London
Tel. 634-4000

Chemical Bank;
180 Strand
London
Tel. 379-7474

Citibank, N.A.
336 Strand
London
Tel. 240-1222

The principal American Express offices are located at:

> 6 Haymarket
> London
> Tel. 930-4411

> 23/31 Waring Street
> Belfast, Northern Ireland
> Tel. 23-03-21

Check with American Express for a complete list of its facilities throughout the country.

Health and Hospitals. There are no vaccination requirements for Americans entering England, except if coming from Asia, Africa, or South America, in which case a smallpox certificate is required.

In the event of medical emergency requiring an ambulance the nationwide emergency telephone number is 999 (which also will summon police and fire authorities if needed).

Americans in need of medical assistance should contact the closest American consulate. The consulate will have a more complete list of hospital facilities, as well as a list of English-speaking doctors and health professionals. (See Section I:2 on U.S. consular services.)

Automobile and Highway Regulations. Americans in the United Kingdom may drive with either an international driver's license or a valid American license.

Beware: In the United Kingdom, all driving is on the left side of the road. Once adjustment is made for left-side driving, handling the automobile in the United Kingdom is generally governed by rules of the road familiar to Americans. However, Americans should be aware of the following special considerations:

- seat belts must be worn
- pedestrians in a "zebra crossing" have the right of way
- children under 14 may not travel in the front seat unless suitably restrained.

Speed limits are typically 30 to 35 mph in towns, 60 mph on the open road, and 70 mph on the highway.

Travel information and assistance may be obtained from the Royal Automobile Club, Pall Mall, London SWI (Tel. 839-7050).

Art and Antiquities. The United Kingdom has restricted the export of certain valuable art objects of the kind detailed below

113

by requiring that an export license be obtained before they can be removed from the country:

- archaeological items (with the exception of coins) which are 50 years old or more and which were recovered from the United Kingdom;
- manuscripts and other documents which are 50 years old or more;
- photographic prints or negatives which are 60 years old or more and valued at 200 U.K. pounds or more;
- any other item valued at 8,000 U.K. pounds or more, and produced 50 years or more before export.

The export license may be obtained from the Department of Trade. If the item is purchased from a gallery or auction house the necessary paperwork will usually be performed by the seller. Generally, the government will grant the license unless the object is deemed a national treasure, and even then the British Museum must match the purchase price. These regulations will usually not present any problem for the American traveler.

Law and Criminal Justice. The United Kingdom is a constitutional monarchy with a democratic parliamentary government. The government and legal system of the United Kingdom are familiar to Americans because we are their direct descendants. Consequently, there are great similarities in our respective approaches to the rule of law—not necessarily in the precise procedures that apply in any particular circumstance, but rather in a shared sense of how the law must function relative to the rights and responsibilities of the individual.

- In the United Kingdom, the decision to prosecute normally rests with the police, although some of the more serious offenses require the approval and participation of the attorney general as well. Typically, the government retains a private barrister to act as prosecutor and present the government's case in court.
- Criminal trials in the United Kingdom are in the form of an adversary proceeding, as in the United States. Except for the less serious offenses tried in the Magistrate's Courts, criminal trials are conducted by the Crown Court before a jury.

The drug laws of the United Kingdom provide for a wide range of punishment for everything from possession to trafficking. As a result, there has been a history of widely divergent sentencing by strict and lenient judges even within the same community. In an attempt to standardize the punishments provided for illegal drug offenses, the Court of Appeals has recently issued a series of guidelines that suggest the following general rules:

- possession of small amounts of marijuana or hashish, though technically subject to a maximum sentence of five years, will usually be punished only by a fine; similarly, importing small amounts for personal use will be dealt with like possession, that is by a fine;
- the larger-scale marijuana offenses are dealt with more severely; for example, the importation of up to 20 kilos (about 44 lbs.) of cannabis will result in a sentence of between 18 months and three years;
- possession of the hard drugs is technically punishable by as much as seven years' imprisonment, but the circumstances of each case, including medical considerations, must determine whether imprisonment is warranted—the court clearly indicated that in may cases only a fine will be imposed;
- the most serious drug offenses involve the importation of, and trafficking in, hard drugs; in such cases, it is seldom that a sentence of less than three years will be imposed.

Because of an increasingly serious drug problem in the United Kingdom, the authorities are especially alert at the borders. Travelers arriving from places known for easy access to drugs, such as Amsterdam, can expect to receive the closest scrutiny.

Although the United Kingdom is one of the oldest and most stable democracies in the world, in recent years it has been torn by the intractable problems of governing Northern Ireland. In order to deal with the violence and terrorism that mark that conflict, the British have enacted special legislation curtailing the legal rights of suspected terrorists, thereby threatening the country's tradition of respect for civil liberties. For example:

- the police may arrest, without a warrant, anyone suspected of being involved in terrorism;
- the person arrested may be detained by the police for as long as seven days for interrogation without being brought before a judge;
- the police may also arrest and detain for seven days anyone who may have information about terrorism, even if the person arrested is not actually suspected of being a terrorist;
- the police may enter and search any place, without a warrant, if they reasonably believe a terrorist may be hiding there.

These provisions will not likely affect most Americans, even those Americans who find themselves in trouble with the law. However, there are a substantial number of Americans who claim to be supporters of the separatists in Northern Ireland and may, as a result, be subject to investigation under these laws.

115

The United Kingdom is a common law country, and the British criminal justice system functions in the common law tradition (as described in Section II:8). Aside from the peculiarities of its antiterrorism laws, some of the particular attributes of the British system of criminal procedure are the following:

- A person arrested by the police must be brought before a magistrate within 24 hours, or in the case of some serious offenses (including drug offenses) as soon as practicable.
- The magistrate will determine whether the defendant may be held in confinement awaiting trial. In making that determination, the court will consider whether the individual is likely to appear at trial and whether the person will engage in any other criminal conduct.
- Bail is a well-accepted procedure in the United Kingdom and is often applied to foreigners as a way of permitting release while also providing some assurance of appearance at trial.
- Although a person in custody is generally permitted to contact a lawyer immediately after arrest, the police have the power to delay notification if necessary to further the investigation or apprehend other criminals.

IV

RETURNING TO THE UNITED STATES

Standing in the customs area of the International Arrivals Building at Kennedy Airport, researching this book, I spoke with a number of Americans returning after a trip abroad. Some were sad the vacation was over; others were thrilled to be home; others were just tired. But everyone had feelings of foreboding about going through customs.

For the most part, such feelings arise from a lack of familiarity with what the government requires of you, the resulting uncertainty about whether you have done anything wrong, and an inability to prepare for what may happen. Every American returning to this country must pass through both an immigration and customs check, and though some delay is unavoidable, the processing can be painless—either because you are lucky or because you know what you are doing.

1. IMMIGRATION AND PASSPORT CONTROL

An immigration check, which is designed to make certain that everyone entering the country has a legal right to be here, is the first thing that happens when the traveler returns to this country from abroad. For the American citizen traveling on a valid passport, the immigration check will be a nonevent.

Typically, passengers will deplane at specially designed international arrivals facilities and be directed through what the government calls a "sterile area"—meaning that there are no exits other than through immigration (and, after that, customs), and no opportunity for the traveler to have contact with anyone already in this country.

Americans with passports are usually separated from the rest of the travelers, and for them the immigration check consists of nothing more than a brief interview with an inspector, who is interested in only two things: Is the traveler the person identified in the passport, and is the passport valid?

The identity check is done by looking at the photograph and, perhaps, asking a few quick questions (such as name, and date and place of birth).

Determining the validity of a passport requires nothing more than checking the expiration date and making a quick examination of the passport itself for signs of tampering. Unless there is a problem, the immigration check can take as little as 30 seconds, and rarely longer than a minute or so.

---

2. CUSTOMS

There is one general rule governing the import of foreign goods into this country from abroad, and it is both simple and comprehensive: *every foreign item obtained outside of the United States is subject to customs declaration and import duty when brought into this country.*

However, to say that everything is "subject" to declaration and duty merely means that the government's power to require declaration and duty is absolute. That is, the government can insist on declaration and duty if it wants. In fact, however, the government has chosen not to exercise that power in certain circumstances. Most importantly, U.S. residents are permitted a limited exemption from that general rule:

> *Generally, each U.S. resident returning from abroad is entitled to a $400 duty exemption—in other words, each resident may return to this country with $400 worth of goods obtained abroad without paying any duty on those goods (subject to certain special limitations on tobacco and liquor).*

Of course, merely stating those general standards does not do justice to the full complement of rules and regulations adopted to implement them. Fortunately for the average traveler, most of these legal details pertain to the intricacies of business transactions and do not generally apply to the average tourist. This is not to say, of course, that rules governing the average traveler are not also complex, for they are. However, these rules are explained below with as much simplicity as accuracy permits.

In studying these customs provisions, keep two things in mind: *First*, these rules change and this compilation is only to alert you to the circumstances that may affect you. *Second*, this is only a simple summary, and if you have any complex customs problem or question you should discuss it with a customs official.

■ THE GENERAL SCOPE OF CUSTOMS CONTROL

Customs control applies to everything obtained abroad and imported into this country. (To some people, the word *import* sounds like a business term. However, import is used in this chapter in a broader sense to mean anything brought into this country from abroad, even if it is a personal item carried in the bag of an individual traveler.) Thus, customs control applies to:

- purchases;
- gifts;
- repairs or improvements to items brought from the United States;
- articles the traveler carries into the United States for another person.

The first aspect of customs control is the obligation to declare imported goods. Every purchased foreign item must be declared. However, depending on the item, and the total dollar value of the imports, it may be sufficient to make an oral declaration to the customs inspector at the time of entry. (The customs declaration procedures are described below.) The second aspect of customs control is the payment of duty (an import tax) on the foreign goods brought into the United States. Since duty (as well as the personal exemption from duty) is based on the value of the item in question, the determination of that value is the first step in assessing duty.

For customs purposes, all goods obtained abroad are to be valued at the price you actually paid. This means that if you got a good deal on an item, and paid less than it might otherwise be worth, your customs obligation is limited to what you paid. On the other hand, if you should obtain a receipt for *less* than the amount you actually paid, your customs obligation is nonetheless the real amount paid. (Customs Service warns, "It is well known that some merchants abroad offer travelers invoices or bills of sale showing false or understated values.") If the item was not purchased (for example, a gift), it will be assessed at the fair retail value in the country where acquired.

One limited exception to the purchase-price rule involves goods that have been used in Europe. If an item is purchased abroad and then used or worn significantly before you return to the United States, duty may be diminished to more closely reflect its current value rather than the original purchase price.

■ RESIDENT EXEMPTIONS.

Each U.S. resident is entitled to import some foreign goods without paying any duty at all. That "personal exemption" works like this:

1. Amount. The amount of the standard personal exemption is $400, which means that an American resident can return to this country with foreign goods worth up to $400 without being required to pay duty.

However, if the trip included stops in the U.S. Virgin Islands, American Samoa, or Guam (even if you traveled to other places as well) then the personal exemption rises to $800 (provided that no more than $400 of that amount represents items obtained elsewhere than in these islands).

2. Applicability. Personal exemption may be applied only to articles acquired for personal use, whether your own or purchased as a gift for someone else. Thus, articles obtained abroad in connection with business, or intended for resale, may not be included as a personal exemption. In addition, foreign goods claimed under personal exemption must physically accompany the traveler returning to this country.

3. Joint Exemption for Families. Personal exemption applies to each U.S. resident traveler, including children (except for the liquor allowance, explained below, which is limited to adults), and families are allowed to combine individual exemptions as a joint family total. Thus, a husband and wife traveling with two minor children are entitled to combine each $400 exemption as family exemption, totaling $1,600. The advantage of joint exemption is that it may be applied to family purchases without regard to which member in the family bought merchandise. For example, if a four-person family returned with $800 worth of clothes for mother, and $800 worth of cameras for father, no duty would be charged, although the parents would have had to pay duty had they been traveling without kids.

4. The 30-Day Limitation. You can only claim a personal exemption once every 30 days, even if you do not "use up" that entire exemption on your first trip. In other words, if you take advantage of all, or any part, of your personal exemption, you must wait 30 days before you are entitled to claim the personal exemption again.

5. The 48-Hour Requirement. A traveler can only claim personal exemption if staying outside the United States at least 48 hours.

6. The $25 Exemption. If you are not entitled to the full personal exemption, because of the 48-hour or 30-day requirements, then you may claim a $25 exemption.

7. Tobacco Products. Only a limited portion of personal exemption may be applied to tobacco products. Each individual (including children) may return duty-free with no more than 100 cigars and no more than 200 cigarettes (one carton).

A person entitled to only the $25 exemption may return duty-free with 50 cigarettes or 10 cigars (or 4 fl. ounces of alcoholic beverage or 4 fl. ounces of perfume containing alcohol).

Note that all tobacco products are subject to state and local taxes. Whether or not the customs authorities collect those taxes, however, depends on the arrangements made with the local authorities. If taxes are due, you can be sure you will be told. More often than not, local taxes will not be an issue.

8. Alcohol. Only a limited portion of the personal exemption may be used for alcoholic products.

The $400 exemption is applicable only if the imported alcoholic beverage:

• is for the traveler's own use, or for a gift;

• is not in excess of one (1) liter (a liter is 33.8 fl. ounces; both a "fifth" and a quart of alcohol, as well as the typical wine, champagne and liqueur bottles, are all less than a liter, and thus are subject to exemption); this rule refers to the total volume of the liquor, not the number of bottles, so that a number of smaller bottles may be applied to the exemption so long as the total contents do not exceed the limit;

• is not in violation of state or local laws. A traveler entitled to the $800 exemption is subject to the same rules, except that a total of four (4) liters of alcohol (135.2 fl. ounces) may be applied to the exemption (so long as no more than one liter is purchased elsewhere than in the U.S. Virgin Islands, American Samoa, or Guam).

A person entitled only to the $25 exemption is also subject to the same rules regarding alcoholic beverages, except that no more than 4 fl. ounces may be subject to exemption.

Note that the liquor allowance may be claimed only if the traveler is 21 years of age or older, even if the state of entry or residence has a lower drinking age (unlike all other items which, if subject to exemption, may be attributed to U.S. resident children).

■ THE PRICE OF DUTY

Of course, you are permitted to bring back items from abroad in excess of your exemption (with the exception of certain prohibited or controlled items). But if you do so, you may be required to pay duty and taxes on the excess.

1. Flat-Rate Duty. After the personal exemption is exhausted, the next $1,000 worth of dutiable articles is assessed at a flat rate of 10 percent. Thus, items valued at $1,400 (the exemption plus the first thousand dollars) are subject to a duty of $100 (that is, no duty on the first $400, and 10 percent on the next thousand dollars). And because a family combines its exemptions and files a joint customs declaration, a family of four can return with as much as $5,600 worth of dutiable items and pay only $4.

2. Variable Duty. If the traveler exceeds the exemption plus $1,000, then the rates of duty prescribed by law become applicable. As of 1983, the Customs Service estimated that this variable rate duty averaged about 12 percent on goods typically imported by travelers. (For the reader's information, the rates of duty for some of the more common items are included in Appendix D). However, the precise rate of duty will be assessed by the customs official at the time of declaration.

Duty must be paid at the time you arrive in this country with the dutiable goods. Duty may be paid with U.S. currency; personal check payable on a U.S. bank; money orders or traveler's checks, but only if they do not exceed the amount of duty by more than $50.

■ GOING THROUGH CUSTOMS

The customs check is the last stop of the trip; the final hassle. It can be anything from a minor inconvenience to a major, frustrating delay. Fortunately, when the traveler finally gets to the inspector, the customs process usually turns out to be considerably less traumatic than had been anticipated, particularly if he has his receipts together and his foreign purchases readily accessible just in case.

The Customs Declaration. When a traveler arrives by commercial airline or ship, Customs Declaration forms will be distributed on board, before arrival. If for any reason the declaration form is not received in advance, it will be readily available at Customs when you arrive. These forms must be completed in advance of passing through Customs.

Everyone must fill out and submit the Customs Declaration form. However, because a returning family is permitted to aggregate its personal exemptions, the family may submit a single joint Customs Declaration on behalf of all family members returning together.

In addition to certain identification questions (e.g., name, address, etc.) and questions of special customs concern (e.g., whether plants or animals are being imported, whether the traveler is carrying large sums of cash), the Customs Declaration form requires the traveler to state the total dollar value of goods acquired abroad.

Generally, the traveler is not required to identify those foreign goods in writing. However, a written listing of foreign acquired goods is required if the total value exceeds $1,400 per person.

Red Line/Green Line. After claiming luggage, and with the Customs Declaration form and passport in hand, you are ready to pass through Customs. In order to speed up customs processing, most international checkpoints have adopted a modified Red Line/Green Line system long common in Europe.

The Green Line is meant for travelers whose purchases do not exceed $800, who are not carrying cash in excess of reportable limits, and who are not importing restricted or prohibited items.

Green Line processing in the United States, however, is considerably different from that usually found in Europe. In Europe, travelers with nothing to declare go through a Green Line that permits passage freely into the country, without customs examination. In the United States, even Green Line travelers may be individually examined by a customs inspector.

Typically, the Green Line inspector will look at the traveler's passport and Customs Declaration form and ask a few preliminary questions such as which countries were visited, how long the trip was, and the like. If the traveler has stated that foreign purchases do not exceed the personal exemption allowed, the inspector will usually ask for a description. If there is any question about the value, the inspector may ask to see either the goods or the receipts, or both.

In the large percentage of cases, the inspector will accept the traveler's oral declaration and permit the traveler to pass through Customs without further inquiry.

Red Line processing is meant for travelers who have duty to pay or special problems to deal with. In particular, travelers must use the Red Line when returning with:

- items in excess of the personal exemption;
- liquor or tobacco in excess of the applicable limitations;
- any fruit, vegetable, plant, live bird, or meat products (or if the traveler had been on a farm abroad);
- $10,000 in currency, or more;
- any commercial articles, samples or goods for business purposes;
- items being carried for someone else;
- items sent home from the U.S. Virgin Islands, American Samoa, or Guam.

Red Line processing proceeds very much like that on the Green Line. The inspector will ask to see the traveler's papers and will question the traveler about declarable goods. An inspector is no more or less inclined to order a full search of a Red Line traveler than of a Green Line traveler; for the most part, the inspectors on both lines rely on the traveler's declaration. Of course, intensified questioning, and even a full search, may be ordered if the inspector becomes suspicious for any reason.

Once your duty obligations have been satisfied, the customs processing is completed and you are officially home.

APPENDICES

A. PASSPORT OFFICES

Boston Passport Agency
Room E123, John F.
  Kennedy Bldg.
Government Center
Boston, MA 02203
24-hour recording: (617)
  223-3831
Public inquiries: (617)
  223-2946

Chicago Passport Agency
Suite 380, Kluczynski
Federal Bldg.
230 South Dearborn
  Street
Chicago, IL 60604
24-hour recording: (312)
  353-5426
Public inquiries: (312)
  353-7155

Honolulu Passport Agency
Room C-106, New Feder-
al Bldg.
300 Ala Moana Blvd.
P. O. Box 50185
Honolulu, HI 98650
24-hour recording: (808)
  546-2131
Public inquiries: (808)
  546-2130

Houston Passport Agency
One Allen Center

500 Dallas Street
Houston, TX 77002
24-hour recording: (713)
  229-3607
Public inquiries: (713)
  229-3600

Los Angeles Passport
  Agency
13th Floor, Federal Bldg.
11000 Wilshire Blvd.
Los Angeles, CA 90024
24-hour recording: (213)
  209-7070
Public inquiries: (213)
  209-7075

Miami Passport Agency
16th Floor, Federal Office
  Bldg.
51 Southwest First Avenue
Miami, FL 33130
24-hour recording: (305)
  350-5395
Public inquiries: (305)
  350-4681

New Orleans Passport
  Agency
Room 400, International
  Trade Mart
Two Canal Street
New Orleans, LA 70130
24-hour recording: (504)
  589-6728

Public inquiries: (504)
589-6161

New York Passport
Agency
Room 270, Rockefeller
Center
630 Fifth Avenue
New York, NY 10111
24-hour recording: (212)
541-7700
Public inquiries: (212)
541-7710

Philadelphia Passport
Agency
Room 4426, Federal Bldg.
600 Arch Street
Philadelphia, PA 19106
24-hour recording: (215)
597-7482
Public inquiries: (215)
597-7480

San Francisco Passport
Agency
Suite 200, 525 Market
Street
San Francisco, CA 94105
24-hour recording: (415)
974-7972
Public inquiries: (415)
974-9941

Seattle Passport Agency
Room 992, Federal Bldg.
915 Second Avenue
Seattle, WA 98174
24-hour recording: (206)
442-7941
Public inquiries: (206)
442-7945

Stamford Passport Agency
One Landmark Square
Street Level
Stamford, CT 06901
24-hour recording: (203)
325-4401
Public inquiries: (203)
325-3538

Washington Passport
Agency
1425 K Street, N.W.
Washington, DC 20524
24-hour recording: (202)
783-8200
Public inquiries: (202)
783-8170

B. PRIVACY ACT RELEASE FORM

American Consulate Athens, Greece
91 Vas. Sophias Avenue

In accordance with the Privacy Act (PL 93-579) passed by Congress in 1974, the Consulate cannot release any information regarding you that is not considered to be in the public domain to anyone without your written consent except as set forth in the Act. Therefore, it is requested that you complete the authorization below specifying whom the Consulate at Athens may contact and release information to with regard to your case. Please return the completed authorization to the Consular Officer or to the address given above.

AUTHORIZATION FOR THE RELEASE OF INFORMATION UNDER THE PRIVACY ACT

I, _____ ,do hereby authorize the Con-
(Your Name)

sulate of the United States of America at Athens, Greece and the Department of State to release information regarding my

_____

(Specify Type of Consular Assistance)

_____

to the following:

A. NAMES AND ADDRESSES OF PERSON(S) YOU WISH THE CONSULATE TO CONTACT

_____
(Name)
_____
(Address)
_____
(Name)
_____
(Address)
_____
(Name)
_____
(Address)

B. IN THE EVENT OTHER PERSONS REQUEST INFORMATION REGARDING MY CASE INFORMATION CAN BE RELEASED TO THE FOLLOWING:

Yes   No   Family (other than those listed under item A)
Yes   No   Friends (other than those listed under item A)

Yes	No	Individual members of Congress
Yes	No	Members of the Press
Yes	No	The General Public

Information will only be released under item B if requested and if we have your authorization.

_____   _____
(Date and Place)   (Individual's Name)

PRIVACY ACT NOTICE FOR USE WHEN REQUESTING INFORMATION FROM U.S. CITIZENS IN CONNECTION WITH CONSULAR SERVICES

The information requested is authorized by 22 USC 2658 and is voluntary.

The primary purpose for soliciting the information is to establish your citizenship, identify, and entitlement to welfare and protection service by the U.S. Government. The information is also needed to assist you in your present need for consular services.

This information may be made available on a need-to-know basis to Personnel of the Department of State and other Government agencies having jurisdiction in the performance of their official duties. If may also be made available to officials of the host government, should the disclosure of such information be considered to be in your interest.

Failure to provide the information requested on this form may make it difficult or impossible for the Department of State to assist you.

American Embassy
Consular Section
Athens, Greece
October 1980

C. EMBASSIES, CONSULATES AND TOURIST OFFICES

Austria

EMBASSY:
2343 Massachusetts
Ave.,   N.W.
Washington, DC 20008
Tel: (202) 483-4474

CONSULATES:
31 East 69th Street
New York, NY 10021
Tel: (212) 737-6400

Wrigley Bldg., Suite 672
410 N. Michigan Avenue
Chicago, IL 60611
Tel: (213) 380-7550

3440 Wilshire Boulevard,
    Suite 910
Los Angeles, CA 90010
Tel. (213) 380-7550

NATIONAL TOURIST OFFICE:
500 Fifth Avenue,
    2009-22
New York, NY 10110
Tel: (212) 287-8742

Belgium

EMBASSY:
3330 Garfield Street, N.W.
Washington, DC 20008
Tel: (202) 333-6900

CONSULATES:
50 Rockefeller Plaza,
Suite 1004
New York, NY 10020
(212) 586-5110

Peachtree Center
Cain Tower, Suite 2306
P. O. Box 56287
Atlanta, GA 30303
Tel: (404) 659-2152

333 N. Michigan Avenue
Room 2000
Chicago, IL 60601
Tel: (312) 263-6624

M. C. 0. plaza
5718 Westheimer,
Suite 760
Houston, TX 77057
Tel. (713) 784-8077

3921 Wilshire Boulevard
Suite 600
Los Angeles, CA 90010
Tel: (213) 385-8116

NATIONAL TOURIST OFFICE:
745 Fifth Avenue
New York, NY 10022
Tel: (212) 758-8130

France

EMBASSY:
4101 Reservoir Road,
    N.W.
Washington, DC 20007
Tel: (202) 944-6200

CONSULATES:
3 Commonwealth Avenue
Boston, MA 02116-2197
Tel: (617) 266-1680

444 N. Michigan Ave.
Suite 3140
Chicago, IL 60611
Tel: (312) 787-
    5359/60/61

100 Renaissance Center
Suite 2975
Detroit, MI 48243
Tel: (313) 568-0990/91

2727 Allen Parkway,
Suite 876

Houston, TX 77019
Tel: (713) 528-2181

8350 Wilshire Boulevard
Suite 310
Beverly Hills, CA 90211
Tel: (213) 653-3120

One Biscayne Tower
33rd Floor
2 South Biscayne Blvd.
Miami, FL 33131
Tel: (305) 379-7641

934 Fifth Avenue
New York, NY 10021
Tel: (212) 535-0100

3305 St. Charles Avenue
New Orleans, LA 70115
Tel: (504) 897-6381/2/3

Mercantile Plaza Bldg.
Suite 720
Avenida Ponce de Leon
Parada 27 1/2 Hato Rey
San Juan, PR 00918
Tel: (809) 753-1700

540 Bush Street
San Francisco, CA 94108
(415) 397-4330

NATIONAL TOURIST OFFICE:
610 Fifth Avenue
New York, NY 10020
Tel: (212) 757-1125

Germany
(Federal Republic of)

EMBASSY:
4645 Reservoir Road, N.W.
Washington, DC 20007
Tel: (202) 298-4000

CONSULATES:
1000 Peachtree Center
Cain Tower
229 Peachtree Street, N.E.
Atlanta, GA 30043
Tel: (404) 659-4760/61/62

100 North Biscayne Blvd.
Suite 1717
Miami, FL 33132
Tel: (305) 358-0290/91

535 Boylston Street
Boston, MA 02116
Tel: (617) 536-4414

104 S. Michigan Avenue
Chicago, IL 60603
Tel: (312) 263-0850

Edison Plaza, Suite 2100
660 Plaza Drive
Detroit, MI 48226
Tel: (313) 962-6526

1900 Yorktown, Suite 405
Houston, TX 77056
Tel: (713) 627-7770

2834 International Trade
  Mart
2 Canal Street
New Orleans, LA 70130
Tel: (504) 524-0356/
  6560

6435 Wilshire Boulevard
Los Angeles, CA 90048
Tel: (213) 852-0441

460 Park Avenue
New York, NY 10022
Tel: (212) 940-9200
  (212) 940-9253 (week-
  ends & holidays)

6th Floor International Bldg.
601 California Street
San Francisco, CA 94108
Tel: (415) 981-4250

1617 IBM Building
1200 Fifth Avenue
Seattle, WA 98101
Tel: (206) 682-4313

NATIONAL TOURIST OFFICE:
747 Third Avenue
New York, NY 10017
Tel: (212) 308-3300

Greece

EMBASSY:
2221 Massachusetts
   Avenue, N.W.
Washington, DC 20008
Tel: (202) 667-3168

CONSULATES:
2211 Massachusetts
   Avenue, N.W.
Washington, DC 20008
Tel: (202) 232-8222

69 East 79th Street
New York, NY 10021
Tel: (212) 988-5500

168 N. Michigan Avenue
Chicago, IL 60601
Tel: (312) 372-5356

2441 Gough Street
San Francisco, CA 94123
Tel: (415) 775-2102

2318 International Trade
   Mart Bldg.
New Orleans, LA 70130
Tel: (504) 523-1167

Tower Place
Suite 1670
3340 Peachtree Road, N.E.
Atlanta, GA 30026
Tel: (404) 261-3391

NATIONAL TOURIST OFFICE:
645 Fifth Avenue
Olympic Tower
New York, NY 10022
Tel: (212) 421-5777

Ireland

EMBASSY:
2234 Massachusetts
   Avenue, N.W.
Washington, DC 20008
Tel: (202) 462-3939

CONSULATES:
515 Madison Avenue
New York, NY 10022
Tel: (212) 319-2555

535 Boylston Street
Boston, MA 02116
Tel: (617) 267-9330

400 N. Michigan Avenue
Chicago, IL 60611
Tel: (312) 337-1868

655 Montgomery Street
San Francisco, CA 94111
Tel: (415) 392-4214

NATIONAL TOURIST OFFICE:
590 Fifth Avenue
New York, NY 10036
Tel: (212) 869-5500

Italy

EMBASSY:
1601 Fuller Street
Washington, DC 20009
Tel: (202) 328-5500

CONSULATES:
690 Park Avenue
New York, NY 10021
Tel: (212) 737-9100

101 Tremont Street
Boston, MA 02108
Tel: (617) 542-0483

500 N. Michigan Avenue
Chicago, IL 60611
Tel: (312) 467-1550

421 Chestnut Street
Philadelphia, PA 19106
Tel: (215) 592-7329

11661 San Vicente
   Boulevard
Suite 911
Los Angeles, CA 90049
Tel: (213) 836-6207

231 Carondelet Street,
Suite 708
New Orleans, LA 70130
Tel: (504) 524-2272

2590 Webster Street
San Francisco, CA 94115
Tel: (415) 931-4925

NATIONAL TOURIST OFFICE:
630 Fifth Avenue
New York, NY 10111
Tel: (212) 245-4822

Luxembourg

EMBASSY:
2200 Massachusetts, Avenue, N.W.
Washington, DC 20008
Tel: (202) 265-4171

CONSULATES:
Permanent Mission of
   Luxembourg to the U.N.
801 Second Avenue
New York, NY 10017
Tel: (212) 370-9850

NATIONAL TOURIST OFFICE:
Same as above

The Netherlands

EMBASSY:
4200 Linnean Avenue,
N.W.
Washington, DC 20008
Tel: (202) 244-5300

CONSULATES:
1 Rockefeller Plaza
11th Floor
New York, NY 10020
Tel: (212) 246-1429

303 East Wacker Drive
Suite 410
Chicago, IL 60601
Tel: (312) 856-0110

Post Oak Bank Bldg.,
Suite 610
2200 Post Oak Boulevard
Houston, TX 77056
Tel: (713) 622-8000

Central Plaza
3460 Wilshire Blvd.
Suite 509
Los Angeles, CA 90010
Tel: (213) 380-3440

712 International Bldg.
601 California Street
San Francisco, CA 94108
Tel: (415) 981-6454

NATIONAL TOURIST OFFICE:
576 Fifth Avenue
New York, NY 10036
Tel: (212) 245-5320

Portugal

EMBASSY:
2310 Tracy Place, N.W.
Washington, DC 20008
Tel: (202) 265-1643

CONSULATES:
899 Boylston Street
Boston, MA 02115
Tel: (617) 536-8740

630 Fifth Avenue
New York, NY 10020
Tel: (212) 765-2980

3298 Washington St.
San Francisco, CA 94115
Tel: (415) 346-3400

1180 Raymond Boulevard
Newark, NJ 07102
Tel: (201) 622-7300

Turk's Head Building,
Room 610
Providence, RI 02903
Tel: (401) 272-2003

628 Pleasant Street
New Bedford, MA 02740
Tel: (617) 997-6151

NATIONAL TOURIST OFFICE:
548 Fifth Avenue
New York, NY 10036
Tel: (212) 354-4403/
4/5/6/7

Spain

EMBASSY:
2700 - 15th Street, N.W.
Washington, DC 20009
Tel: (202) 265-0190

CONSULATES:
545 Boylston Street,
Suite 803
Boston, MA 02116
Tel: (617) 536-2506

2411 Fountainview,
Suite 130
Houston, TX 77055
Tel: (713) 783-6200

180 N. Michigan Avenue,
Suite 1905
Chicago, IL 60601
Tel: (312) 782-4588

6300 Wilshire Boulevard
Suite 1431
Los Angeles, CA 90036
Tel: (213) 658-6050

2325 Salzedo Street
Coral Gables, FL 33134
Tel: (305) 446-5511

2101 International Trade
Mart
#2 Canal Street
Tel: (504) 525-4951

150 East 58th Street
New York, NY 10022
Tel: (212) 355-4080

Avenue Condado 605,
Oficina 521
Condominio San Alberto -
Quinto Piso
Santurce, PR 00908
Tel: (809) 724-0533

2080 Jefferson Street
San Francisco, CA 94123
Tel: (415) 922-2995/6

NATIONAL TOURIST OFFICE:
665 Fifth Avenue
New York, NY 10022
Tel: (212) 759-8822

Switzerland

EMBASSY:
2900 Cathedral Ave., N.W.
Washington, DC 20008-
3499
Tel: (202) 745-7900

CONSULATES:
307 N. Michigan Avenue
Chicago, IL 60601-5369
Tel: (312) 782-4346/
4074/4075

3440 Wilshire Boulevard,
Suite 817
Los Angeles, CA 90010-
2176
Tel: (213) 388-4127/9

1920 International Trade
Mart
New Orleans, LA 70130-
1398
Tel: (504) 525-0164/
524-7081

444 Madison Avenue
New York, NY 10022-6981
Tel: (212) 758-2560

235 Montgomery Street
Suite 1035
San Francisco, CA
94104-3090
Tel: (415) 788-2272

Allied Bank Plaza, Suite
5670
1000 Louisiana
Houston, TX 77002
Tel: (713) 650-0000

NATIONAL TOURIST OFFICE:
608 Fifth Avenue
New York, NY 10020
Tel: (212) 757-5944

United Kingdom

EMBASSY:
3100 Massachusetts
Avenue, N.W.
Washington, DC 20008
Tel: (202) 462-1340

CONSULATES:
225 Peachtree Street, N.E.
Suite 912
Atlanta, GA 30303
Tel: (404) 524-5856/8

4740 Prudential Tower
Boston, MA 02199
Tel: (617) 437-7160

33 North Dearborn Street
Chicago, IL 60602
Tel: (312) 346-1810

1650 The Illuminating Bldg.
55 Public Square
Cleveland, OH 44113
Tel: (216) 621-7674

Dresser Tower, Suite 2250
601 Jefferson
Houston, TX 77002
Tel: (713) 659-6270

813 Stemmons Tower
West
2730 Stemmons Freeway
Dallas, TX 75207
Tel: (214) 637-3600

321 St. Charles Avenue
10th Floor
New Orleans, LA 70130
Tel: (504) 586-1979

701 Wilshire Boulevard
Los Angeles, CA 90010
Tel: (213) 385-7381

845 Third Avenue
New York, NY 10022
Tel: (212) 752-8400

NATIONAL TOURIST OFFICE:
40 West 57th Street
New York, NY 10019
Tel: (212) 581-4700

D. SELECTED LIST OF DUTY ON COMMON TOURIST PURCHASES—1984 [1]

	General Duty	Duty on Goods from Communist Countries
ANTIQUES produced prior to 100 years before the date of entry	Free	Free
BAGS, hand, leather (not over $20)	10%	35%
BEADS:		
Imitation precious and semiprecious stones	4.7-17.2%	40-100%
Ivory	6.3%	45%
BOOKS, foreign author or foreign language	Free	Free
CAMERAS:		
Motion picture, over $50 each	5.1%	20%
Still, over $10 each	4.7%	20%
Cases, leather	7.4%	35%
Lenses	8.8%	45%
CANDY	7%	40%
CHESS SETS	5.9%	50
CHINA TABLEWARE:		
Bone	11.6%	75%
Nonbone Valued not over $56 per set	30.7%	75%
Valued over $56 per set	11.9%	75%
CIGARETTE LIGHTERS:		
Pocket, valued at over 42% each	9%	110%
Table	7.5%	60%
CLOCKS:		
Valued over $5 but not over $10 each	46¢ each + 10% + 3.9¢ each jewel	$3 each + 65% + 25¢ each jewel

135

	General Duty	Duty on Goods from Communist Countries
Valued over $10 each	45¢ each + 6.4% + 2.5 each jewel	$4.50 each + 65% + 25¢ each jewel
DOLLS AND PARTS	14.1%	70%
DRAWINGS (works of art) done entirely by hand	Free	Free
FLOWERS, artificial, plastic	13.1%	60%
FRUIT, prepared	7%	35% or under
FUR:		
Wearing apparel	7.4 - 11.6%	50%
Other products of	3.4 - 7.4%	50%
FURNITURE, Wood, chairs	6.5%	40%
Wood, other than chairs	3.4%	40%
GLASS TABLEWARE	15 - 42.5%	60%
GLOVES:		
Not lace or net, plain vegetable fibers, woven	25%	61%
Wool, over $4 per dozen	26/lb. + 13%	50¢/lb. + 50%
Fur	6.2%	50%
Horsehide or cowhide	15%	25%
GOLF BALLS	3.8%	30%
HANDKERCHIEFS:		
Cotton, ornamented	.2 each + 7.5%	53.5%
Cotton, plain	26% + 3/lb.	67.5%
IRON, travel type, electric	3.4%	35%
IVORY, products of	4.9%	35%
LEATHER:		
Pocketbooks, bags	8.1 - 10%	35%
Other products of	1.5 - 10%	35%
MAH-JONG SETS	5.92%	50%
MUSICAL INSTRUMENTS:		
Music boxes, wood	5%	40%

	General Duty	Duty on Goods from Communist Countries
Woodwind	5.9%	40%
PAPER, products of	4.5 - 6.5%	27 - 40%
PEARLS: Loose or temporarily strung and without clasp:		
Genuine	Free	10%
Cultured	2.3%	10%
Imitation	12.5%	60%
Permanently strung (with clasp attached or separate)	17.2%	110%
PERFUME	3/lb. + 5.9%	40¢/lb. + 75%
RADIOS:		
Transistor	7.7%	35%
Other	5.9%	35%
RATTAN furniture	13.9%	60%
RECORDS, phonograph	4.2%	30%
SHOES, leather	8.5 - 10%	20%
SKIS and **SKI EQUIPMENT:** Ski boots	6.2% 8.5 - 10%	33.3% 20%
STONES, cut but not set: Diamonds	Free	10%
Other	Free - 3.4%	10 - 20%
TAPE RECORDERS	4.2%	35%
TELEVISIONS	4.2%	35%
TOYS	10 - 10.9%	70%

1 The duty on imports changes with sufficient frequency to warrant a note of caution that the figures in this chart are for purposes of general information, and may not be applicable at the time you pass through Customs. Current duty rates on any particular item can be obtained by calling the nearest Customs Service Office.
2 Any product manufactured or produced in certain Communist countries — even if purchased by you in Western Europe — is subject to an increased rate of duty.

INDEX

141